AN INTRODUCTION
TO THE WORLD OF WORK

AN INTRODUCTION
TO THE WORLD OF WORK

DAVID SPURLING

authorHOUSE®

AuthorHouse™ UK
1663 Liberty Drive
Bloomington, IN 47403 USA
www.authorhouse.co.uk
Phone: 0800.197.4150

Published by AuthorHouse 02/17/2016

ISBN: 978-1-5049-8982-4 (sc)
ISBN: 978-1-5049-9023-3 (e)

Print information available on the last page.

Any people depicted in stock imagery provided by Thinkstock are models,
and such images are being used for illustrative purposes only.
Certain stock imagery © Thinkstock.

This book is printed on acid-free paper.

NASA Earth Observatory image by Robert Simmon, using Suomi NPP VIIRS data provided courtesy
of Chris Elvidge (NOAA National Geophysical Data Center), April and October 2012

Contents

Personal Modules

Topic	Index Reference
Module P1 Shopping	
Food shopping	P1.10
Detergents and Wash Balls	P1.20
Loyalty Cards	P1.30
Project on Loyalty Cards	P1.40
Buy Two get One Free	P1.50
Project on Buying in Bulk	P1.60
Market stalls	P1.70
Project on food buying	P1.80
Project on Refrigerators	P1.90
Clothing	P1.100
Footwear	P1.110
Project on Footwear and Clothing	P1.120
Computers and Printers	P1.130
Project on Computers and Printers	P1.140

Topic	Index Reference
Module P2 Healthy Eating	
What do we need for a healthy diet?	P2.10
Packaged Foods	P2.20
Eating Out	P2.30
Fluids	P2.40
Sell by Dates	P2.50
Having an adequate sized Freezer or Refrigerator	P2.60
Is fast food bad food?	P2.70
Pasta	P2.80
Pulses	P2.90
Cooking several items at a time	P2.100
Cooking larger quantities and using them later	P2.110
Other quick healthy foods	P2.120

Topic	Index Reference
Module P2 Healthy Eating (cont.)	
Recipe for an omelette	P2.130
Herbs and other flavourings	P2.140
Project	P2.150

Topic	Index Reference
Module P3 Budgeting	
Setting a budget	P3.10
Project on Budgeting	P3.20

Topic	Index Reference
Module P4 Travel	
Rail travel	P4.10
Coach fares	P4.20
Cycling	P4.30
Motorcycles and Mopeds	P4.40
Cars	P4.50
Car sharing	P4.60
Project on travel	P4.70

Topic	Index Reference
Module P5 Fuel Bills	
Fuel Bills	P5.10
Cooking	P5.20
Computers	P5.30
Freezers and Refrigerators	P5.40
General methods of cutting down electricity bills	P5.50

Topic	Index Reference
Module P6 Patterns of expenditure	
TV and Entertainment	P6.10
Theatres and Cinemas	P6.20
Project on CPI	P6.30

Topic	Index Reference
Module P7 Accommodation	
Bed and Breakfast	P7.10
Unfurnished Accommodation	P7.20
Project on Accommodation	P7.30

Business Modules

Topic	Index Reference
Module B1 Office work in different sectors of a business	
Office work	B1.10
Primary Industry	B1.20
Secondary Industry	B1.30
Manufacturing	B1.40
Tertiary Industry	B1.50
Project on occupation	B1.60
Project on paperwork	B1.70

Module B2 Office planning	
Why plan an office?	B2.10
Location of the office	B2.20
Desirability of the office	B2.30

Module B3 Reception office	
Role of the reception office	B3.10
The virtual office (instead of reception)	B3.20
Project on the effectiveness of the reception office	B3.30

Module B4 Telecommunications	
Number of Phones	B4.10
Advantages and Disadvantages of phone systems	B4.20
Knowledge of local Phone Codes	B4.30
Phone packages	B4.40
Different phone systems	B4.50
Project on Telecommunications	B4.60

Topic	Index Reference
Module B5 Mail	
Inward Mail	B5.10
Outgoing Mail	B5.20
Project on Mail	B5.30

Topic	Index Reference
Module B6 Private sector organisations	
Sole Traders	B6.10
Project on Catering	B6.20
Partnerships	B6.30
Private companies and Public Limited Companies	B6.40
Franchises	B6.50
Project on Franchises	B6.60
Workers Cooperatives	B6.70
Consumers' Cooperatives	B6.80
Project on Cooperative Shops	B6.90
Project on Cooperative Banks	B6.100
Non-profit-making private sector organisations	B6.110
Project on Types of Organisations	B6.120

Topic	Index Reference
Module B7 Business risks	
Risk takers	B7.10
Project on Looking at a Market	B7.20
Insurance	B7.30
Project on honesty of employees	B7.40
Project on Vehicle Insurance	B7.50

Topic	Index Reference
Module B8 Growth of organisations	
Internal and External Expansion	B8.10
Project on Takeovers	B8.20
Vertical Integration Backwards and Forwards	B8.30
Lateral integration	B8.40
Reasons for wishing to grow	B8.50
Project on Road Haulage vehicles	B8.60
Managerial Economics	B8.70
Project on large and small firms	B8.80
Diseconomies of scale	B8.90
Project on organisational charts	B8.100

Topic	Index Reference
Module B9 Production methods	
Unit Production	B9.10
Batch Production	B9.20
Mass Production	B9.30
Flow production	B9.40
Project on Mass Production	B9.50

Topic	Index Reference
Module B10 Human Relations Department	
Wages and Salaries	B10.10
Queues	B10.20
The Workplace	B10.30
Project on efficiency	B10.40
Project on annual reports	B10.50
Recruitment	B10.60
Project on Recruiting	B10.70

Topic	Index Reference
Module B11 Accounting	
Purpose of Accounting	B11.10
Project on Taxis	B11.20
Project on Financial scandals	B11.30

Topic	Index Reference
Module B12 Finance	
Importance of finance	B12.10
Methods of finance	B12.20
Project on finance	B12.30
Project on setting up a dance club	B12.40
Public sector	B12.50
Project on central government	B12.60
Project on local authorities	B12.70
Case study on a road haulage business	B12.80

Topic	Index Reference
Module B13 Purchasing	
Reasons for purchasing	B13.10
Project on your own purchases	B13.20
Stock Control	B13.30
Project on ice cream vans	B13.40

Topic	Index Reference
Module B14 Marketing	
The importance of marketing	B14.10
Marketing segments (young people)	B14.20
Marketing segments(older people)	B14.30
The four P's (Product, Price, Place and Promotion	B14.40
After sales service	B14.50
Government persuasive advertising	B14.60

Topic	Index Reference
Module B15 Distribution of goods	
What is distribution?	B15.10
Project on loaves	B15.20
Supply Chains	B15.30
Online shopping	B15.40
The importance of distribution	B15.50
Project on the high street	B15.60
Project on electrical goods	B15.70
Containers	B15.80
Project on containers	B15.90

Topic	Index Reference
Module B16 Organisations and methods	
What is O and M?	B16.10
Project on Doctors	B16..20

Topic	Index Reference
Module B17 Sources of information	
The information age	B17.10
Public libraries	B17.20
Project on Eastern Europe	B17.30
Dictionaries	B17.40
Wikipedia	B17.50
Books shops	B17.60
Project on new words	B17.70
Project on errors	B17.80
Project on dictionaries and thesaurus	B17.90

Topic	Index Reference
Module B18 Business Meetings	
Importance of meetings	B18.10
Project on success of meetings	B18.20
Project on using a meeting to publicise your organisation	B18.30

Topic	Index Reference
Module B19 Arranging visits	
Arranging travel	B19.10
Overseas Visits and Documentation	B19.20
Knowledge of other cultures and languages	B19.30
Project on visiting emerging economies	B19.40

Topic	Index Reference
Module B20 Looking for jobs	
Training for work	B20.10
Project on your career	B20.20
CV	B20.30
Example of a CV	B20.40
Example Reference 1	B20.50
Example Reference 2	B20.60
Project on CV's	B20.70
Project on higher education	B20.80
Project on interview techniques	B20.90
Obtaining work at the present time	B20.100
Project on local jobs	B20.110
Suggested letter to accompany CV to prospective employer	B20.120
Module B21 Specimen interview with Miss Smith	
Your Business Studies Course	B21.10
Your background	B21.20
Word-processing and IT skills	B21.30
Your role and future	B21.40
Minor Conditions	B21.50

Module P1 Shopping

The supermarket chains
In the United Kingdom the large supermarket chains such as Sainsbury's, Tesco, Morrisons and ASDA have dominated the food market. They are not necessarily the cheapest places to buy food, despite their massive advertising and also their price comparisons with each other. Aldi and Lidl have gained ground considerably since the credit crunch from 2008 onwards. This is because they are thought to be cheaper than the others.

Other supermarkets
There are other supermarket chains including The Co-operative, which as its name suggests is owned by the customers, and also Waitrose which is owned by the workers and is part of the John Lewis group.

Waitrose has a reputation for selling good but more expensive products than other supermarkets. The idea about higher prices is not necessarily true so it is worthwhile looking at these supermarkets. Waitrose has the advantage that often they are located near railway stations or other public transport so is somewhat easier to get to than some of the other major chains. Many of the other larger supermarkets are now located on out-of-town sites which means that when looking at the total bills we need to think of the cost of getting there as well as the time taken.

Value for money
It is important when shopping to compare like with like. For example, juice drinks often have far less fruit in them than pure fruit juice so if you are looking at the fruit juice content, then compare the percentages. You can always add water if you need it. Similarly some drinks such as squash (which will be diluted), have a much higher percentage of fruit so you need less of it in the first place.

P1.20 Detergents etc
The same applies to non-food buying including washing-up liquids, sometimes you have to use far more of some brands than others.

It is environmentally better and cheaper in the long run to use wash balls rather than detergent although the initial cost is quite high.

Own brand labels

The supermarkets offer their own brand labels which are often cheaper than the better-known brands offered by the giant food firms. They often also offer a value product under different titles which is similar to the idea of the no-frills airlines.

The reason for buying unbranded goods, sometimes called own label goods, is simple. You are not paying for the huge amounts of advertising.

Aldi has shown the extent of this price difference by showing a typical basket of food and other household items with the well-known brand labels and then comparing this with the typical basket of Aldi foods and other items.

P1.30 Loyalty cards

The major supermarket chains also offer loyalty cards which give discounts according to the amount purchased. From the student viewpoint these are worthwhile having since they reduce the cost of shopping.

They issue loyalty cards so they can build up a picture of the purchasing habits of their customers. Supermarkets will call this customer profiles. Sometimes, rather than swapping the discounts for cash, they may offer reductions on prices at tourist attractions which may give better value.

In some towns smaller shops have sometimes banded together to give their own loyalty cards which give discount in a number of different shops.

P1.40 Project on Loyalty Cards
Make a list of the different loyalty cards which are available from both Boots and the supermarkets.

What rewards do they give and what percentage is this of the total price?

In some cases the loyalty cards give discounts for tourist attractions or for computers, travel etc. How much would you have to spend in order to get these discounts, for example how much money would you need to spend to get an airline ticket?

They try to appeal to people's better nature, for example by giving vouchers for school equipment. Show how much people need to spend before the receiving organisation could gain anything substantial.

How could smaller organisations such as shops in a small town try to compete against the larger shops and why might some people prefer to use them?

P1.50 Buy two get one free

There is also the possibility of collective shopping, often with offers of buy two get one free or buy one get one free which may not be suitable for a single person household. However, students may be able to buy two or three and then share them afterwards.

This type of pricing has been criticised, as in the U.K. It has been estimated that a third of all food which is in the supermarket distribution chain is wasted partly because people buy what they regard as a bargain and it then goes mouldy in the refrigerator or food cupboard.

P1.60 Project on Buying in Bulk
Make a list of the items in the supermarket or other shops where they sell items more cheaply, if you buy several rather than one.

Which of these items would it be possible to keep for consumption later, for example water filters or soap and which would be difficult to store for example perishable fruit or vegetables?

From this information list which of these might be helpful to a single person household and which would be only suitable if there are several people in the same household.

Sometimes the supermarket receipt may give an indication of the total savings from these offers.

Is the savings a significant part of your total bill and is there any way that you could get together with other people to make more savings in this way.

P1.70 Market Stalls
In some cases food which is near the end of its sell by date can often be obtained more cheaply. This is even truer for market stalls which still rely heavily on the idea of "sell them cheap pile them high". There are far fewer market stalls than there were. Market stalls often sell fruit and vegetables which are much cheaper than in the typical supermarket or other shops.

In many cases also they sell a wider variety of cheeses and sometimes meat than in the typical supermarket at much cheaper prices.

Often fruit and vegetables are cheaper in the season because they are bought from local sources. This will be in contrast to other produce which has to go to London wholesale markets and then back to the local area. The distribution costs have to be paid and this is going to be reflected in the price.

It is noticeable that in many cases people from the ethnic minorities will often gather around just before the close of a market since they know that the prices will drop at this time of the day.

P1.80 Project on Food Buying
Make a list of the foods which you eat during the week. This will include fresh food as well as tinned, frozen food, fast food and possibly meals out.

Check the prices of these in terms of the well-known brands and the value brands and classify them according to where you could buy them.

If possible, plot them on a graph or bar chart which you should be able to do in Excel or any computer program.

What do you notice about the range of prices?

Does this give you any guidance as to what is the best place to buy food?

P1.90 Project on Refrigerators and Freezers
Make a list of the items which you keep in the refrigerator. Do the items vary according to the time of the year?

How long do the different items remain in the refrigerator?

Why might this be important to know?

Do you find that keeping such a list helps you to avoid wasting food?

In what ways could this help you to know whether to buy larger or smaller quantities of food when there are special offers?

P1.100 Clothing

Clothing can be a large part of total expenditure. In many cases charity shops offer a wide variety of clothes, often at bargain prices and also you know that you are doing good at the same time.

Some charity shops are much better than others at displaying material. A little research may be needed before deciding on which ones offer the best quality clothing for the prices.

It is important to have rainproof garments for either leisure or business purposes. You may well have seen on television people in remote areas when snow has been forecast struggling with inappropriate clothing. Equally shower-proof clothing is not very helpful.

This is not very helpful if you are in an area where there is likely to be torrential rainfall. In particular it is unhelpful if you're just going for an interview. There have been examples where the weather forecasters have forecast snow and yet people have totally inappropriate clothing if their car gets stuck.

Online Shopping

Online shopping may be helpful when buying clothes since people of one extreme size may have an easier experience finding items. It is probably not so helpful when buying shoes when correct fitting is necessary if one wants to avoid storing up problems in the future.

P1.110 Footwear

Footwear is important and is one of the items you need to be very careful when buying since poor footwear can lead to accidents or sometimes to long-term damage to the feet which cannot necessarily be healed.

Whilst style might be thought to be important, clearly it is much more important to have footwear which is practical. In particular if you are going to be out in bad weather then it is important that you have suitable footwear which will not lead you to trip over.

It is often helpful and cheaper to repair shoes than simply to discard them.

One of the advantages of repairing shoes is that the shoes will mould to some extent to your foot so they may be more comfortable than buying new shoes. If you have to discard shoes, there are often clothes banks which will take old shoes.

P1.120 Project on Footwear and Clothing
Look at your wardrobe. How many items in it have you bought and only used infrequently?

Where do you buy clothes? Is it local shops, market stalls, the nearest big town, online, charity shops ? Is your shopping pattern typical? If not, why? Make a survey of your friend's clothing and footwear and buying patterns. Do they find that buying more expensively means better quality and longer lasting products?

P1.130 Computers and Printers

Whilst most people buy new computers it is often possible to buy refurbished computers quite cheaply which will still have sufficient RAM and ROM for most purposes. These are often much cheaper than buying a new one and unless you need to impress people for some reason there seems to be no reason to buy a more expensive model.

In spite of the so-called paperless office, most people still do print material in which case laser printers can be advantageous.

P1.140 Project on Computers and Printers
Look at the prices of a range of different computers with the specifications which you might consider acceptable, then look at the price of refurbished computers including ones you can buy direct from the seller.

Also look at the cost per page of printing with a variety of different printers both colour and monochrome. Show on a bar chart how much it would cost if you printed 10 copies, 100 copies or 1000 copies per week.

P1.150 online shopping
Online shopping has the advantage for consumers that it minimises transport costs and time. It can be very helpful for disabled people. However, it means that last-minute bargains of perishables is not possible. Another disadvantage is that not all firms either guarantee a convenient time slot or keep to them. Sometimes it may be sensible to group together with others to take advantages of offers such as buy two get one free. This minimises the problems of hanging around waiting for deliveries.

Module P2 Healthy eating

P2.10 What do we need for a healthy diet?
We need to think of the basic needs for a balanced diet e.g. protein, fibre, carbohydrates, some fats, minerals, and the different vitamins as well as calories etc. The UK Chief Medical Officer has advised that five portions of fruit and vegetables should be eaten every day.

How much food do we need in total?
We need to think how many calories we actually need; around 2000 for women and 2500 for men per day. This does however vary considerably according to the amount of exercise which people take; clearly Bradley Wiggins would need a lot more. Bradley Wiggins won the Tour De France as well as an Olympic medal in 2012.

It will also depend upon the type of job that we do, hard manual work will mean that we need more calories than if we are working in an office.

P2.20 Packaged Foods
Most packaged food nowadays shows the amount of fat, calories etc and although it is time-consuming it is worthwhile checking that we are having a healthy diet.

This information could be set out on a spreadsheet so that we can look at the total calories, vitamins, fat and proteins that are being taken in over a period. This helps to check that we are having a sensible diet.

P2.30 Eating Out
Food eaten out on the other hand does not necessarily show the number of calories that are being consumed and even what might look like healthy food, such as a salad may have so much dressing that the food is not healthy.

Eating out tends to be much more expensive but may be necessary. In some well-publicised fast food places you are paying really for the advertising. Many restaurants and cafés do offer a student discount so that if you have to eat out, it is worthwhile making a note of when these discounts apply.

P2.40 Fluids
There are different amounts of fluid which people require according to age and gender. Dehydration can lead to problems including double vision.

Many drinks, including soft drinks as well as alcohol, have a considerable number of calories. One possibility is simply to drink more water. Another alternative is to make one's own drinks such as tea and coffee since these are often quite expensive when you eat out, even if the basic meals are not too expensive.

It is also possible to make one's own lemon drink (recipe shown below) which, whilst it has a number of calories is both cheap and far less harmful than many others.

Lemon Drink Recipe
Ingredients
4 medium sized lemons
400ml of water
100g of sugar

Peel and squeeze the lemons with a lemon juicer. Add the peel to the juice and add about 400ml of water and pour on boiling water and add 50g of sugar per lemon. Leave for 24 hours and then consume.

Bottled Water
Bottled water is an unnecessary source of expenditure and in 2012 there were press reports about two large supermarkets who had simply sold tap water in bottles, but at inflated prices.

Any undesirable chemicals can be reduced through using a filter and this will be considerably cheaper, (about 1p per litre) than even the cheapest forms of bottled water.

P2.50 Sell by dates
There is a need to be aware of sell by dates. Some of these are frankly ridiculous; it is difficult to understand why salt has a sell by date. On the other hand some meat (especially pork) and fish (especially shellfish) can lead to food poisoning if it is not consumed at the right time. There has been some concern in the UK that people have completely ignored sell by dates to reduce their expenditure.

P2.60 Having an adequate size freezer or refrigerator
If you're living in rented accommodation it may be worthwhile thinking of the advantages of having a freezer or refrigerator. This means that slightly larger quantities of food can be bought at cheaper prices and if the fridge is used sensibly this avoids wasting food.

In many cases 4 pints of milk are much cheaper than buying individual pints, and if accommodation is shared then this is easy to use.

P2.70 Is fast food bad food?
Fast food does not have to be bad food, for example jacket potatoes are both cheap and nutritious.

These can be done in a microwave oven in around about 10 minutes although some people prefer them if they are done in an ordinary oven. A compromise may be to do them in a microwave for a few minutes and then to finish them in an ordinary oven.

If people are eating the skin itself which is nutritious there is no waste at all and the only time taken in preparation is to make sure that the jackets themselves are scrubbed.

P2.80 Pasta
Pasta which can be known under a variety of different names such as spaghetti, cannelloni, macaroni, and penne, forms part of the staple diet for many southern European countries, and is widely used in this country. It can be part of a cheap nutritious diet in this country and will form an alternative to chips.

P2.90 Pulses
Pulses include peas and the various types of beans which can be found in nearly all food shops.

Even baked beans are both nutritious and cheap if one can buy a version with minimal salt and sugar.

Pulses are a good form of nutrition; again it is often quite easy to find the so-called basic items called by different names in different shops.

P2.100 Cooking several items at a time
Take notice of how long it takes to cook items and you can therefore use some form of chart.

Item	Cooking Time
Potatoes	30 minutes
Chicken	20 minutes per 400g plus 20 minutes additional cooking time
Peas	10 minutes

Therefore if we have a meal for 4 with the chicken taking 2 hours, if we want to have the meal at 12.30 we would need to put the chicken in at 10.30, the potatoes in at 12.00 and the peas in at 12.20.

P2.110 Cooking larger quantities and using them later
In some cases it is worthwhile (as with rice pudding) making up considerable quantities which can then be eaten up over time, this saves cooking time as well as energy.

P2.120 Other quick healthy foods
Omelettes are also easy to do and can be used as a cheap base for a variety of fillings. This could be either savoury which is the most common or sweet as in the case of bananas which is a good way of using up any mushy bananas.

P2.130 Recipe for an Omelette
Ingredients
3-4 eggs for two or three people
Small amount of butter or margarine

Break the eggs into a basin. If you want a slightly lighter omelette you can add a few drops of water. Whisk the eggs until it is a consistent mixture.

Melt enough butter or margarine to cover the bottom of the frying pan, do not use low-fat margarine since this may spit and cause a mess.

Cheese Omelette

If you're making a cheese omelette wait until the omelette is almost set before putting in the cheese since otherwise the cheese will tend to be rather stringy.

Spanish Omelette

You can make a Spanish omelette by using a variety of fillings such as tomatoes, especially cherry sized ones as well as other ingredients such as mushrooms.

Banana Omelette

If you are making banana omelette which is a good way of using up over ripe bananas then wait until the omelette is almost set before stirring in mashed bananas.

P2.140 Herbs and other flavourings

Herbs have traditionally been used both to give flavouring and also to help to reduce certain symptoms.

Some herbs are expensive but they can be grown fairly easily in a small space if this is available. Packet herbs are more expensive if branded and in many cases it is possible in whole food shops to get them more cheaply.

Root Ginger looks very strange but is obtainable from market stalls and other outlets and can add a considerable amount of taste to otherwise bland food. The same is even truer of chillies.

P2.150 Project

Many supermarkets as well as other firms use loss leaders. These are items which are sold below costs. Clearly they cannot sell all items at a loss. If people come to buy these basic items (conventionally milk or sugar), people will buy many other items whilst they are there so that overall the supermarket makes a large profit. Firms sometimes now use fruit and vegetables as their loss leaders.

Either by visiting the shops or possibly by watching television advertisements, make a note of which items are publicised regularly. Explain briefly why people might visit the supermarket to make these purchases. If possible, when visiting a supermarket see what other items people purchase.

Module P3 Budgeting

P3.10 Setting a budget

If you are away from home and have not been used to setting yourself a budget it may be sensible to either use Excel or even a very conventional word processing package to set out both outgoings and any sources of income.

Budgeting will obviously vary if you are living in your own family house, flat sharing, having a flat of your own or living in a guest house. Setting a budget is helpful and it is a good idea to see why after a month your budget doesn't exactly match with your original ideas. Accountants use the term variance to describe this difference. Below is an example, if oversimplified, budget; you could use it as a basis for your own budget.

Jan	Feb	Mar	Apr	May	June	July	Aug	Sept	Oct	Nov	Dec
Gas			Gas			Gas			Gas		
								PC Insurance			
Phone	Phone	Phone	Phone	Phone	Phone	Phone	Phone	Phone	Phone	Phone	Phone
	Electricity			Electricity			Electricity			Electricity	
Food	Food	Food	Food	Food	Food	Food	Food	Food	Food	Food	Food
Travel		Travel	Travel		Travel			Travel			Travel

We mentioned "buy one, get one free" in "P2 healthy eating", and the same idea applies to other goods and services.

Hint: You may find that it does not just apply to groceries but also to communications such as TV and broadband packages where sometimes firms advertise very low rates for the first few months, relying on people not to switch after this period.

Non-food shopping

Markets may also offer clothes and household items that are much cheaper than in the conventional shops.

P3.20 Project on your expenditure

Keep a notebook of what you buy for a suitable time period such as a month.

Classify the goods and services into the main categories which you find helpful for example food, washing materials, fuel, communications, and travel. Using a suitable computer program (if possible), draw up a pie chart or other suitable method of presentation and compare the data over a period.

Economists sometimes use the phrase seasonal variations. Do you find that your outgoings vary according to the time of year? Is it worth buying some seasonal food when cheap, and storing it in a freezer until a later date?

Module P4 Travel

If you are studying full time at a College which you cannot reach from home, then travel at the start and the end of terms can be expensive. For some students the daily travel to and from College or work can be expensive.

P4.10 Rail Travel

There are offers for cheaper train travel for students which can often reduce the price for travelling to and from home whereas car insurance is often very expensive. It is worthwhile in many cases having the student Rail card which offers a considerable discount. In the United Kingdom this is one third off the standard fare.

In spite of media coverage about rail fares if you book in advance rail fares can often be very cheap and in the south-east of England there are also group fares for three or four people which make travelling much cheaper. There are a variety of different organisations for advanced railway fares but the one that the author has found most helpful is Chester Le Track (0191 387 1387) where you actually speak to a real person although you have to book generally seven days or more in advance. They do not charge any extra for credit cards which sometimes puts up the charges quite considerably.

P4.20 Coach Fares

Similarly coach operators sometimes have special deals especially if tickets are bought in advance.

Young Persons Coachcard
You know you wanna ... save money
Get discount coach fares with the Young Persons Coachcard; for only £10 you can buy a Coachcard and get cheap coach tickets with a discount of **up to 30%.** Whether you're travelling to see your mates or a student popping home from university so mum can do the laundry!

The Young Persons Coachcard is cheaper than a rail card, has no off-peak restrictions, which means you can travel any time. Plus it's easy to buy and you don't even have to send us a photo! As long as you're aged between 16 and 26, or a full time student you are eligible

So what are you waiting for? Apply for your Young Persons Coachcard now and start saving.

Using your coachcard couldn't be easier
Once you have bought your coachcard, getting discounted tickets is easy. Simply book your ticket online in the normal way, remembering to tick the box 'I have a coachcard'. You can also use your

coachcard to book at your local outlet or by calling our Customer Services team on 08717 81 81 78 (calls cost 10p per minute plus network extras). We'll book your journey and automatically give you the discounted fare. Just remember to show your Coachcard AND your ticket when you board the coach

Things you should know
1. Provided the card has not expired, bears the holder's name and signature and is properly used, the card entitles the holder only to travel at the current discount fare on National Express Coach services in the UK (excluding Northern Ireland). Certain inclusive packages, special offers, Funfares and Apex fares are excluded.
2. The card entitles the named holder, or someone acting on his/her behalf, to purchase travel tickets for use by the named holder only at the discount fare.
3. The card is not refundable. National Express reserve the right to invalidate the card of any cardholder who is deemed to be misusing it.
4. A valid card is required for each leg of the journey being made. If a card expires between the outward and return dates, the return journey will not be eligible for the discount fare.
5. Always carry your card and proof of age when travelling, you may be asked to provide it. Without it, you may not be allowed to board the coach.

P4.30 Cycling
Cycling is healthy and in spite of some stupid drivers the insurance companies know that it is likely to lead to a longer life compared with people who take very little exercise.

There are often cycle paths which are much safer than the roads and in towns the journey times may be as quick by bike as they are by car. Cycle helmets should be worn.

Some firms have a loan scheme whereby you can borrow money in order to get a suitable bike.

Folding bicycles can be taken free of charge on trains. Other bicycles sometimes need to have reservations.

In London it is possible to hire bicycles at several stations for a small charge, although it may be free for the first 30 minutes.

P4.40 Motorcycles and Mopeds
Mopeds and Motorcycles have the advantage of a cheaper initial price and good fuel consumption compared with cars. The insurance premiums can be high for younger people.

P4.50 Cars
Cars are usually expensive to buy although mechanically minded people might wish to buy second hand cars. Insurance premiums are very high for young people generally.

P4.60 Car sharing
If car journeys have to be made then it may be helpful to advertise any possible car sharing arrangements which can be done on many college notice boards about the travel that is being made so that car sharing becomes a possibility.

Taxi sharing at the beginning of or end of the terms is also a possibility.

P4.70 Project on travel
Make a note of all the travel which you do during the course of the year whether this is walking, cycling, driving or using public transport. What are the total costs and what is the total time involved? Are there any ways that you can see that could reduce the costs and/or time? Put your data into a spreadsheet.

Module P5 Fuel Bills

P5.10 Fuel bills

If we look at expenses we will see that fuel bills can be quite considerable especially in older property. Lighting is part of the bill (obviously this can be reduced by more energy efficient bulbs which might be worthwhile buying even if the landlord did not do so). Natural light will obviously help reduce the fuel although this might be offset by slightly higher heating bills.

Double glazing is usually expensive to install but thicker curtains or curtain linings will also help to reduce fuel costs. These can often be obtained cheaply from charity shops.

Unless one is buying one's own property or on a long term lease, the choice of energy may be limited but there are a number of ways of trying to reduce the bill.

P5.20 Cooking

One possibility of trying to reduce fuel bills is to ensure that, for example, the oven may be used for several different dishes at the same time.

Microwaves may help to reduce fuel consumption although they are clearly very energy intensive for the time they are on.

Pressure cookers may also reduce the amount of electricity.

With conventional cooking, it is possible to cook several vegetables at one time using a suitable steamer. Slow cookers can also be advantageous and it is possible to cook several items at the same time.

P5.30 Computers

Computers also consume considerable volumes of electricity so if they are not already there it is worthwhile looking at the energy efficiency of different computers.

P5.40 Freezers and refrigerators

Freezers and refrigerators are also major consumers of electricity and it is worthwhile looking at the energy rating of these if they have not already been installed.

P5.50 General Methods of cutting down electricity bills

There are ratings up to A plus and since in many cases running costs of an appliance are much higher than the original purchasing cost, it is therefore worthwhile looking at the use.

Not leaving appliances on standby will also considerably reduce the amount of energy being used and from a safety viewpoint it is also sensible to turn off most items at the mains overnight.

Using showers rather than baths may also reduce the amount of fuel being used.

P5.60 Different prices at different times

Many electricity companies have complicated tariffs but in many cases they offer a discount in the off-peak hours, typically midnight to 7 a.m. It is worthwhile taking advantage of this for activities such as using washing machines or dishwashers providing that this is not going to disturb you or your neighbours. It is also worthwhile recharging any appliances such as razors, mobile phones, hand-held games, iPods etc to take advantage of this cheaper rate.

P5.70 Project on appliance costs

Find out from the Internet or other sources what the running costs of appliances are? Which are the most important when it comes to looking at your fuel bill?

How might this help you if one of your machines is coming to the end of its life and you are deciding whether or not to have a replacement, and if so what should replace it?

P5.80 Project on overall domestic fuel costs

it is possible to reduce fuel costs substantially through loft insulation, cavity insulation, heat extractors, solar panels and thermodynamics.

Using information from the fuel companies including both the larger ones and Good Energy find the total costs of each of these and what grants if any are available from sources such as local authorities.

From this information estimate the likely rate of return from each of the measures mentioned.

Module P6 Patterns of expenditure

P6.10 TV and entertainment
Most students will want some form of television. Freeview, which gives a wide choice of channels, is generally cheaper than paying for a more expensive package to one of the major suppliers.

P6.20 Theatres and Cinemas
Many theatres and cinemas have cheaper admission for students on production of a valid student card. Additionally, some theatres and cinemas have standby tickets which means that seats are not guaranteed but prices are low if you are prepared to take a chance.

P6.30 Discount Schemes
Students often get discounts at restaurants and shops upon showing their student card. Some towns, such as Faversham in Kent, have their own loyalty cards to encourage the use of local independent businesses. Cartridge World also have a discount card.

P6.40 Project on CPI
The consumers prices index (CPI) is one method of measuring inflation. The government looks at the point of expenditure to see how much is spent on different items.

How much of £1000 expenditure is spent on each item?

Item	Expenditure
Food and non-alcoholic beverages	£112.00
Alcoholic beverages and tobacco	£42.00
Clothing and footwear	£65.00
Housing, water, electricity, gas and other fuels	£144.00
Furniture, household equipment and maintenance	£61.00
Health	£24.00
Transport	£162.00
Communications	£27.00
Recreation and culture	£134.00
Education	£19.00
Restaurants and hotels	£114.00
Miscellaneous goods and services	£96.00

Look at the government statistical data and see what is included in the consumer price index (CPI) in more detail and also the retail price index.

Explain why you think that this may or may not be typical of the students that you know and also why it might not be typical for your own household. Then plot your own expenditure for a year if possible and see how it compares with the typical household expenditure for the country as a whole.

Module P7 Accommodation

Many Universities have halls of residence which have some advantages. Though the initial price may sound expensive, they are likely to be well heated and insulated compared with rented accommodation.

Before making a decision it is worthwhile checking what facilities are shared and what restrictions there are, e.g. timings for using the bathroom and whether the kitchen is shared.

P7.10 Bed-and-breakfast

This is usually an expensive form of accommodation but can be helpful if you are in a new area so that you have then time to look around slightly more before making a decision about other forms of accommodation. Some students don't wish to cook and clean.

P7.20 Unfurnished accommodation

The obvious problem with this is that there is often an initial expense in terms of providing suitable furniture such as beds as well as a comfortable seat or settee.

The British Heart Foundation often has good value furniture at reasonable prices and you also know that you're contributing towards a very valuable charity. They also often sell quality television sets, DVD players etc which may well be helpful when setting up for the first time. Some people like the idea of unfurnished accommodation since they can plan the rooms as they want.

P7.30 Project on accommodation

Make a list of the accommodation which is available in your area, subdivided into the relevant categories, for example furnished accommodation, unfurnished, halls of residence etc.

Look at the different costs but also take into account the travel costs and time to wherever you are studying. Then do a thorough analysis of the advantages and disadvantages of the different types of accommodation. You could subdivide this into the comfort or otherwise of the accommodation, the total cost for the period, other features which might not be so easy to quantify such as is the accommodation quiet, moderately quiet, noisy at particular times of the day, which is unlikely to be conducive to people studying.

	Rating	Other Comments
Comfort (1 most comfortable - 5 least comfortable)		
Size of rooms (1 biggest – 5 smallest)		
Quiet/Noisy (1 quietest – 5 noisiest)		
Rent/Lease cost per week (1 cheapest – 5 most expensive)		
Shared bathroom/toilet		
Shared kitchen		
Garage space or space for bikes		
Travel costs (1 cheapest – 5 most expensive)		
Travel time (1 quickest – 5 longest)		
Shower/Bath/Both		

Module P8 Allocation of time

P8.10 Passive activities

Many students as well as the general population are very passive, spending time on the internet, watching TV and playing computer games. People do need relaxation time but it is important to have a sense of balance and socialisation and exercise are important. Allowing time for meals especially breakfast is also important.

P8.20 Allocation of time for study

Allocation of time is important and it is helpful to try to avoid leaving essays or other work until the last minute. This may be easier said than done.

It's important to know your own characteristics e.g. when is the best time to study and whether it is done better in short bursts or for longer periods of time. In some cases it is possible to do some household tasks whilst listening to a radio programme on current affairs etc. This may be helpful for studying at the same time whilst doing other routine household jobs such as the washing up, peeling vegetables etc. Solar powered radios have the great advantage of portability as well as giving no electricity costs. If you are studying current affairs subjects, Radio Four is extremely helpful.

P8.30 Time for Projects

Coursework is a component of many courses, but project management is an essential business tool. If you have a choice of projects it is often helpful to formulate this in the form of a hypothesis. For example, "Does age, gender, social class, or ethnic group, influence the time taken to carry out physical tasks?" It is also often helpful then to subdivide this into further questions. You then need to work out whether you are going to use primary research e.g. asking or observing people directly, or using secondary research e.g. seeing what other studies have already been done. In both cases you need to allocate time, for example, how long will it take to interview enough people and what happens if you cannot find the people quickly enough?

P8.40 Project on Writing Projects

Suppose you hear that a local organisation e.g. a Steel Mill is about to close and you wish to suggest alternatives for the site and also how people could use their transferable skills. Clearly this is a massive project, so you need to split it down into relevant parts. This could be as any part of the steel plant could be feasible to be used for some part of steel production. Could the government subsidise the steel mill if it is a short run problem, and this is not against international rules? As the steel mill is very large are there any alternatives for the site, such as a massive leisure or shopping complex? Do the current workers and managers have any constructive ideas on what could be done?

Activity	Time Allocated	Comments
Allocate time to formulate suitable hypothesis.		
Allocate time to design a questionnaire if necessary.		
Allocate time to carry out interviews.		
Allocate time to analyse data.		
Allocate time to present data.		
Allocate time to check your work.		

P8.50 Homework

When you're doing any homework or other work have an idea of how many words you can write in a time period. Also make a note of your writing speed. Try to work out what your thinking speed is so that you have a fairly clear idea of what you can do within the time frame. Also remember that in most cases you have analysis, application, knowledge and evaluation as the marking criteria. In many cases evaluation is the difficult one to get the marks on.

P8.60 Taking Examinations

At the end of an exam leave a bit of space between different paragraphs so that if you think you can add one thing later you have the opportunity to do this. If you have to add material try and do arrows to indicate where the material is going otherwise it is going to give a bad impression to the examiner.

In most examinations you're entitled to say right at the beginning what points you are going to cover. This can be useful both to you and to the examiner since it helps to give you a structure. For most of us this is the difficult part. It also means that if you have any spare time at the end you can check back to ensure that you have covered these points. Even if you have to write in a note form at the end you will probably still be given credit for this.

P8.70 Project on activities

Keep a diary for a week or a suitable period. Make a note of the different activities which you do for example studying, eating, watching television, using the internet, socialising, playing computer games etc.

Present the information in the form of pie charts or bar charts. Then see how you could become more efficient bearing in mind both financial and emotional needs. It's easy to become addicted to certain things such as computer games and analysis might help you realise how you could become a more effective student. Also make a note of how much of the time you are active and how much time you are passive. One of the concerns of the government not just in this country but in many others is the problem of obesity which is partially caused by lack of activity.

Are there any ways that you can become more active mentally or physically without putting too much stress upon yourself?

If you keep the diary for a longer period which may be advisable then you might notice how changes occur perhaps according to the seasons.

Activities	Intellectual activity (1 using brain all the time – 5 couch potato)	Physical activity (1 most active – 5 least active)
Cooking		
Watching TV		
Using the Internet		
Socialising/Drinking		
Eating		
Computer games		
Washing		
Walking		
Watching Sport		
Reading		
Sleeping		
Other activities		

Module P9 Personal Finance

P9.10 Bank Account
If you do not already have a bank or building society account you may need an account even if it is in effect a piggy bank. There are a wide range of financial institutions.

It is worthwhile looking at the financial pages of newspapers such as The Guardian, The Times, The Daily Telegraph or The Independent. You might use websites which give an insight into the amount of money and the amount of interest which is payable to students if any.

Large shops such as Marks and Spencer and Tesco also provide their own banking service.

There are now apps and online services available for viewing bank account balance and expenditure.

P9.20 Borrowing
It is worthwhile looking at the true rate of interest since the 'friendly' sources of credit can often be very high around 25% to 30% whereas there are cheaper ways of borrowing money than this. In some cases borrowing money (for example though the so-called money shops) can be extremely expensive. True rates of interest have been over 4000%. The financial pages may be very helpful. It may be worthwhile postponing the expenditure rather than having to borrow at such high rates.

In finance some methods of borrowing money are much more expensive and much more risky than others. People have discovered with the credit crunch that borrowing money against property is not necessarily a good way forward even if cheap.

Some towns have Credit Unions which mean that people co-operate to lend each other money at much cheaper rates than are usually obtainable from the banks. (See the Wikipedia website for more information about these).

P9.30 Phone bills
It is worthwhile looking at the costs of a landline if this is available compared with the various mobile packages. Then work out which is the appropriate one for you as an individual.

If accommodation is shared then having a landline with an itemised phone bill may be much cheaper than any other method.

P9.40 Project on personal finance
Look at the different rates of interest on the following.

	Conditions of lending	Security required
Authorised overdraft		
Unauthorised overdraft		
Loans		
Money Shop Loans		
Credit Union Loans		
Building Society Mortgages		
Bank Mortgages		
Store cards		
Credit cards		
Others		

What do you notice about the different rates of interest or yield? Why do people use some of these methods which have no obvious merits?

	Rate of interest	Comments
Current accounts		
Bank current accounts		
Building society current accounts		
Post office accounts		
Preference shares		
Debentures		

Module P10 Self development

P10.10 Self-esteem

Self-esteem is important but not if it is at the expense of other people. The slogan "be nice to people on the way up because you may need them on the way down" has some truth in it.

Low self-esteem may arise for a number of different reasons. These may include worries about appearance, feeling ashamed of the way that you speak, not wishing to be different.

Keeping smart will not make people beautiful or handsome but will help to improve self-confidence. Brushing your hair, wearing clean clothes, cleaning your teeth may all help.

There is no reason to change your accent but there is no reason to speak in sloppy English.

Speaking clearly unless there is a speech defect is not too difficult, for example to pronounce the word butter so that the two ts are clearly heard.

If this is not done especially at interviews, it will lead to a greater chance of rejection. It will also make it more difficult in many cases to sell goods or services.

In extreme cases, if you are totally lacking in confidence, then counselling may help.

Walking tall such as striding rather than dawdling into a room may help to give more confidence.

P10.20 Listening may be as important as speaking

Whilst many books and articles talk about becoming a speaker, perhaps more important is the ability to listen. If there is a conversation either with a group or with an individual then you should try to follow on.

It is not difficult to practice listening and setting oneself individual tasks to show whether your listening is improving can be helpful.

If you have a page of text which you need to learn then try to see how many of the main facts you can remember. Set yourself a target to try to improve each time in the same way as an athlete might try to set themselves time targets.

Remember to think about other people's self-esteem as well, so it is important for those people that you remember their names and also any details which they might have given you. Make a note in a diary or your phone discreetly if possible.

If people come from a different area or different country try to find out something about this area, perhaps either by direct questioning or from the Internet. It then becomes much easier to have conversations which flow. This will help both you and the other person to have more self-esteem.

Regular exercise is important for a variety of reasons including reducing obesity. It also often helps to improve concentration since there is a link between physical and mental well-being.

In many parts of the country there are "Walk and talks" which means that people take a walk with the intention of meeting other people at the same time. A good group leader tries to make sure that no one is left so that even the shyest person will usually find someone to talk to. These walks are usually free so it is a cheaper way of getting exercise than many others.

Most people have a variety of roles for example within the family; sometimes this may involve being a carer for either the old or the young.

P10.30 Different family groups and self-esteem
Caring for the young can be both very time-consuming and also leave people feeling isolated.

In the smaller nuclear family (a nuclear family is one with Mum and/or Dad and siblings) it is often more difficult to involve other family members. In some cases there are semi-formal family groups which may be worthwhile belonging to and in some cases there are "good parenting" groups.

If these do not exist it may be worthwhile mixing with other people in similar circumstances, which means the children still need looking after but that it becomes less lonely and often leads to greater self-esteem. Similar considerations apply to people looking after the elderly.

If one needs to be on call but is not doing anything else it may be a good opportunity to study.

P10.40 The importance of friendship

Friendships outside the family are also important. It is important to distinguish between acquaintances and friends. There is no clear-cut definition but most people would regard friends as people who they could ask for advice on almost anything, whereas this would not be true of acquaintances. Friendships can last a lifetime without interaction. Without social interaction many people will become bitter and it becomes easy to lose perspective and self-esteem.

P10.50 Project on self-esteem
Make a list of the friends that you have. What characteristics do you have in common? Is it a liking for a particular activity such as sports or entertainment? Would you categorise your friends as all being extrovert i.e. outward looking or all introvert i.e. inward looking?

If you change your location perhaps because you are looking for a different job or study elsewhere or simply because your parents move, does the above list help you in any ways to suggest how you might reasonably be able to find new friends? Would social networks such as Twitter, Facebook and LinkedIn help you to find new friends, or are they too impersonal?

Module P11 Relationships

We think of teamwork in sports, such as football, but teamwork is important in ordinary life as well as in business. The ability to work as part of a team is extremely important whether one is working in a shop, factory or office.

Some courses require teamwork. This might apply in a social science course for example looking at an old disused railway track and seeing what could be done with it. This might require different academic subjects, for example knowledge of Law will be helpful to check on legal constraints, knowledge of engineering to find out what is technically feasible and a knowledge of Economics,Business or Accounting to check what is likely to be commercially feasible. Working with people from different backgrounds is very helpful.

It may well be worthwhile trying to go on such courses since emotional intelligence in many cases is more important than pure intelligence. There are a number of techniques to improve teamwork which may include making notes of people's names and their position when being introduced, or even checking up on people's websites.

Emotional intelligence is how well people get on with other people. Unless people are working in a back office entirely on their own, emotional intelligence is obviously very important.

If you are looking for work and know of other people in the same situation, then demonstrating your teamwork for example working in a voluntary capacity with other people, may help.

P11.20 Project on attending meetings
If you are at a meeting where there are discussions going on and if it is appropriate make a note of the social interaction. Does the person speaking reply or follow on from the previous speaker? Does the person totally ignore what was previously said? If the person answers what was said, is it said in a constructive or destructive way?

Module P12 Presentation skills

P12.10 Presentation at meetings

Whilst some people love being the centre of attention and these people will usually be extroverts, many other people get very worried about presenting information. If you are asked to do this it is worthwhile knowing the circumstances for example are there other speakers on the same topic? Nowadays many people go to business meetings (B2B is the jargon which stands for business to business). At these, people from different organisations are often asked to speak for a very short time (possibly 1 minute) on their business. Sometimes apprentices have been asked to do this, perhaps partly to make a change from the typical middle aged men or women at these meetings. It is important to be well prepared to make sure that you don't run over the time limit. If you have a microphone on your computer it is worthwhile seeing how many words you can fit into this time. Then go through the words seeing whether the main points have been made. Could the words be made punchier to use the jargon?

P12.20 Telephone techniques

It is surprising that in many cases people when answering the telephone do not give either their name or (if this is appropriate) the name of the organisation for which they are working.

It is better to say "David Spurling, Learning Through Cooperation Ltd 01795 435 385" as then people will know that they have got through to the right organisation. Similarly if the call is an outgoing one and people are not there, it is very helpful to make sure that both the name and the phone number where one can be contacted are given if this is relevant.

P12.30 Public speaking

It is worthwhile if you have to do public speaking to have some notes. It is not usually helpful to read these out loud since it will come across as very stilted.

It may be helpful to record yourself practicing your speech, e.g. with a smart phone, Dictaphone or memo recorder. You can then listen to the recording to pick up not merely whether the speech is well done, but also how the tone of voice comes across. You should then see whether it can be changed slightly to make it sound friendlier, if this is appropriate.

Speed of speaking

People who are very nervous often speak too quickly or sometimes very slowly. The speed of speech is important. You can get an idea of this by listening to a speaker on radio or television and seeing who comes across in a competent manner.

Use of conversational style
It is often helpful to think of speaking in terms of a conversation rather than to think of it in terms of the number of people you are addressing. You do not need to get too self-conscious about this since we all make mistakes.

How many points are we trying to make?
We do need to however, think how many points we can make within a time period and most newcomers to public speaking make the mistake of trying to get across too much information.

Gapped Handout
Sometimes people have used what is called a gapped handout, where the main points are written on a sheet of paper leaving the listeners with a good framework but also with an incentive to listen to any discussion on these points. If you're the sort of person who might wander away from the main points it does prove a useful check to ensure that you are keeping to the ideas. The same ideas can be used using PowerPoint or any other method where we have the main points, which helps both listeners and the speaker to keep to the main points. Writing out all the ideas on a handout on the other hand seem to be self-defeating since unless you're a very good speaker, why should anyone bother to listen?

P12.40 Project on Business advice
You are working for a small business which specialises in training people for business administration. The business sees an opportunity to concentrate on employability. It has produced a course on this for NEETs (not employed, in education or in training); the course however may also be suitable for people returning to work. Typically these would be mothers or occasionally fathers returning to work after having been carers for children or sometimes parents or other elderly relatives. The firm has asked you as a young apprentice how they can make these courses more appealing to younger people. What advice would you give them?

Module P13 Careers including apprenticeships

P13.10 Exam results may help to get you interviews

In the United Kingdom and many other countries, employers, particularly since the credit crunch, will often have far more applicants than they have places for many jobs, so in order to reduce the number of people they might see they will look initially at exam results. This is called a sifting process.

Even if you fail an exam, you will still have gained some knowledge. In some cases it may be possible to take a lower level examination showing that you have achieved something. If you have a skill and no examination certificates, it may be worthwhile taking an exam if it is not too expensive to do so, either in time or money.

This could well apply to ICT where many organisations ask someone to be computer literate. To have an examination certificate showing this might give you an edge over a person who hasn't.

P13.20 Project on Apprenticeships
You are currently studying business administration and asked to an interview for work with a writer. What questions would you expect him to ask you about the relevance of what you are doing? This suggests that because you are young that you have more idea of what advertising material/social networking might appeal to younger people. Explain how you might try to produce some Facebook, LinkedIn, YouTube and Twitter material which would encourage people to read his books rather than other people's.

What advice would you give him about the length of time which your chosen extract should last? Would you just choose to have him speaking directly with the advantages of him talking to younger people? Would it help to have a number of young people with him or to have just one or two? Would they need to be the same people throughout the presentation? Would it help if this information was on YouTube? How could you use your own social networking group to help publicise the organisation?

P13.30 Project on Apprenticeships using the International Association of Book-keepers (IAB)
If you look at the IAB website, you will see that it offers a variety of courses and also that it is accredited in England by the Office of Examinations and Qualifications Regulator (Ofqual). Why might this be important for both British and overseas students? What do you notice about the news which is on the website? Why might colleges wish to use the qualifications to offer to prospective students? Hint: Look at the fees charged compared with many other bodies.

Module P14 Enterprise and risks

What is meant by being enterprising? This means looking all the time for opportunities to improve the organisation whether it is one's own business, working for a profit-making firm or a charity or working for local or central government.

P14.10 Enterprising schools and colleges
We can see vast differences in different schools even when they have similar students. Some will try to take care of all the students whereas others will only cater for a few.

Some are really trying to make the best use of their buildings for example by hiring their premises out in the evenings and also during the holidays so that they are really part of the community. Some schools have playing fields or swimming pools which can be hired out to the local community. Some schools allow rooms to be hired out in the evenings and others allow foreign language students and others to make use of the premises in the summer and other holidays. This both helps to produce a better community as well as reducing other problems as occupied premises are less likely to get break-ins or fires.

P14.20 Risks
Businesses clearly involve risks especially where we have uncertainty in an age where communications, demand for goods and services and entertainment patterns change rapidly. Public houses try to get more business by having large screen televisions where typically men but some women can watch sports events. Pubs may also sell snacks and meals since this has the advantage of utilising the premises and often reduces rowdyism. If you go to such premises it is worthwhile analysing what is happening and in what ways they are successful and how you think they might improve their facilities.

P14.30 Calculation of risk
Where risks can be calculated fairly precisely it is often possible to have insurance. Employers' liability is compulsory so if you work full or part time, there should be a notice displaying a certificate of employer's liability. There are a variety of different insurance policies including fire policies, life insurance policies, marine insurance and vehicle insurance.

P14.40 Minimising risks
Physical risks can be minimised through sensible procedures and this would apply to safety of electrical appliances as well as to risks of falls etc. The Institute of Advanced Motorists offer courses which can be very helpful.

Risks of wrong calculations of demand

In some cases it is possible to have experiments before launching a full-scale service. We can also relate this to the product life-cycle. For more details on this, see the Principles of Business and Management textbook by David Spurling, John Spurling, James Gachihi and Simon Cruickshank.

P14.50 Career risks

The entertainment business is renowned for having high wages and salaries for successful people. It is easy to find data about this for successful footballers in the media virtually every day, especially where footballers are coming to the end of a contract. However, in many cases the footballers in the lower divisions will not have very high wages and there is a risk of injury which can stop promising careers. It is important therefore if young people are joining a Development Centre for football that they continue to study at the same time. Many actors spend a great deal of their time 'resting' which really means that they are unemployed. It is therefore important that they have a full back position i.e. being able to find other work when this happens.

P14.60 Enterprising

The ability to adapt in most jobs is very important partly because of changes both in products and services, as well as the customers. Different ethnic groups as well as different age groups may well require different products and services and firms serving both local and national markets may have to take account of this.

P14.70 Project showing risks of setting up a dance organisation

Imagine that you wish to be an entrepreneur and wish to enter the party music business. What information would you require before attempting to start this? Would it be sensible to observe what the rivals are doing in your locality and also to look for any gaps in the market? What data could you obtain about the number of young people in your area? Hint: The election register may be useful since all 18 year olds should appear on this unless they are from outside the European Union. You could make a chart showing the prices which they charge and any variations. For example, some will charge less for early entry and more after midnight. How do the clubs try to publicise themselves? Do they, for example, hand out leaflets with discounts if you hand in the vouchers? Do they advertise on local radio or in the local press?

Module P15 Planning in an age of change

P15.10 Example of high street changes

One thing which is reasonably certain is that there is a need to allow for changes in the future. This applies almost irrespective of the business concerned. You can see at the present time the changing nature of the high street in most towns. Previously safe jobs, for example working as a shop assistant are no longer secure. Similarly, working for a high street bank is no longer a secure option.

Online Shopping

Online shopping has become much more important which alters the nature of both shops and the distribution pattern.

There is a niche for small shops and businesses but they often have to adapt to achieve this. For example one shop may advertise it doesn't just sell boxes to people who want to buy new television sets and computers, but will help people to install them as many people find the new technology very difficult to use effectively.

Music industry changes

We know that the music industry has changed rapidly from the vinyl records of the 1980s to tapes and CDs and later DVDs and now downloading of music in a variety of forms. It is almost impossible to guess what will happen to the music industry over a longer period.

P15.20 Project on a small TV, radio and phone shop

You have been working in a small shop which specialises in providing a service for customers who often find digital change difficult to cope with. When they see their television screen, it flashes up messages such as "There is a renumbering of the channels. Do you want to have these channels kept?" Your firm has been willing for a comparatively small fee to install the new televisions and to advise customers on what they need so that it has not told them to go for an expensive package if a cheaper one is available. The market is changing rapidly as the collapse of Comet showed in 2012, so that some former customers have now decided to take advantage of the more personal service which your firm has. How would you try to publicise your organisation? How can you encourage people to recommend your organisation, for example would a discount of 10% the next time they use your organisation help? Can your organisation enter competitions to become the best new business in the local newspaper competition? Would it help to belong to the local chamber of commerce?

Module B1 Office work in different sectors of a business

B1.10 Office Work

What is office work?
Nearly all businesses and organisations whether they are working for profit, are voluntary organisations or are part of local and central government will have paper work to do and this is often referred to as office work.

Market Traders
Let us look at one of the simplest businesses for an example. Market traders will have to know what prices they are paying and what prices they are charging. If they do not do this they are likely to land up having unwanted goods at the end of the day. Market traders will need to pay income tax and therefore need to keep a note of how much money they have spent and how much money they have paid for the goods they are selling. A lot of information however will be kept in the trader's head including having knowledge of their customers' shopping habits. Market traders often sell fruit and vegetables, or sometimes meat and fish, and rely on being able to sell them cheaply but in large volumes. They can also be flexible about their pricing policy, so they will mentally store this information without much paperwork.

Large-scale businesses
Large-scale businesses generally will have much more paperwork. Although this phrase is still used, much of the information is computerised. Such information is usually called data on the computer.

In the United Kingdom far more people now work in offices (which is part of the tertiary sector) than work in either the primary sector or the secondary sector.

B1.20 Primary Industry
Primary production is the production of raw materials. It includes extractive industries, such as coal mining and the oil extraction industry, and also includes agriculture, fishing and forestry.

In the United Kingdom, a small percentage of people work directly in the agricultural industry.

The government wishes to have a greater proportion of land devoted to forestry, but recent problems caused by ash dieback disease show that this may not be as simple in practice.

There have been concerns about over-fishing which has depleted stocks of fish. Many people would like to see a more sustainable fishing policy. At the present time, a great deal of fish which have been caught are thrown back dead into the sea as they do not match the dimensions which are allowed to be caught. The European Union is currently altering its Common Fishing Policy.

Fracking, a source of fuel, is a new but controversial industry.

B1.30 Secondary Industry

The construction industry is dominated by large scale firms. In 2012 the government tried to boost employment in this sector by reducing planning regulations. There are however, still many small firms in the building trade, often doing repairs and minor building works such as extensions rather than building complete houses. In some cases insurance companies will employ smaller building firms if there are repair jobs to do.

Engineering is important. In November 2012 the government announced that it wanted to see more infrastructure such as the building of new railways including a high speed link from London to Birmingham, Yorkshire, Lancashire and Scotland. Engineering would also be important for other major rail projects such as the Crossrail project and the electrification of the railway line from Paddington to Bristol, Cardiff and Swansea. The electrification of the valley lines in Cardiff could help to regenerate the area.

B1.40 Manufacturing

Manufacturing is still important to the United Kingdom although the numbers of people working in it have decreased.

B1.50 Tertiary Industry

The tertiary sector is sometimes referred to as the service sector and has been the fastest growing sector in the UK. However the credit crunch from 2008 onwards meant that many people have been concerned that there are far too many people working in sectors such as the banks. The banks have been shown to have little integrity. The tertiary sector includes: banks and building societies; the National Health Service; and education, whether primary school, secondary school or university. It also includes distribution.

The distribution industry, which is large, includes people working in warehouses, as lorry drivers, on the railways, in the merchant Navy, and at airports.

The National Health Service is still one of the largest employers in the United Kingdom but is undergoing major changes at the present time. The emphasis is intended to be changing from focusing on treating sickness to trying to help people to keep fit in the first place. However, the credit crunch has meant that people are eating more processed foods because they are apparently cheap. This leads to more obesity in the first place.

The education sector is a major one. The government requires people to stay on at school until the age of 18, but alternatives such as technical colleges, home tuition, and apprenticeships, are available. A large proportion of young people now go on to higher education, although the number may decrease slightly among those from poorer backgrounds, with people being deterred by the publicity about tuition fees.

B1.60 Project about occupations

If you are in touch with people who were in the same year as you at school do an analysis of which occupations they are in by classifying them as to whether they are mainly involved in office work, manual work, etc.

How could you present this information, for example in terms of a pie chart, bar chart? Which is the easiest to understand?

If people had the choice why have they chosen a particular occupation? Why might attitudes as well as aptitude be important?

B1.70 Project on paperwork

If you are in touch with teachers or lecturers ask them about the paperwork which they have to do, but beware of violent reactions!

- What is the logic of having to carry out risk assessments every time the teacher has to take students out?
- Ask if having a vast amount of paper in the state sector schools but much less in the private sector academies help anyone?
- Ask what information they would require about potential students?

B1.80 Self-examination Questions

Q1) Give 2 examples of occupations which are in the primary sector, secondary sector and tertiary sector.

Q2) What paperwork (if any), do we need in order to obtain vehicle insurance? What paperwork would we need in order to buy textbooks from Learning Through Cooperation Ltd? What paperwork would we need in order to register for the IAB examinations?

Q3) Using the appropriate websites if possible, look at the number of people employed in the primary, secondary and tertiary industries. What do you notice about the trends?

Module B2 Office Planning

B2.10 Why plan an office?

With the credit crunch many firms are reviewing the costs of running their offices. This includes both the running costs - which include telephones, computers and staff - as well as the rent or lease. There are also business rates in the UK, which can be very high per unit area (e.g. per square metre) in areas such as central London.

In order to attract new businesses, some local authorities have developed business centres for them offering incentives such as free office space to all starter businesses trading in their first year since registration. They sometimes also offer serviced offices meaning new small businesses that will often not be able to afford a full time secretary but may wish to have secretarial facilities as and when it is required, are catered for. In some cases, they may also have a small area which can be hired on an hourly, half-daily or daily basis which can be used if an organisation wishes to have a larger area for a reception or for publicity purposes. They may also provide free Wi-Fi.

B2.20 Location of the office

Many firms are also considering relocation partly because of changes in the population. Organisations will usually wish to be in an area where the population is increasing rather than decreasing, and unless staff are working from home, organisations want to be accessible to a large number of potential staff. In some cases the offices may be near the factory or depot so there may be little choice. The rising costs of fuel means that some firms are adopting green plans which means that they want stakeholders whether managers, staff or customers to be able to travel easily to the office. This may be particularly important in cities such as London where car parking is restricted and congestion high so that using public transport, cycling or walking would be better.

B2.30 *Project on desirability of the office*

Either from your present job, or if you are not currently employed, look at potential offices where you might be employed in the future. Make a table using the following features.

Name of Location	Yes/No	Comments
Is it easily accessible by foot?		
Is it easily accessible by bike?		
Is it easily accessible by bus?		
Is it easily accessible by train?		
Is there adequate car parking for customers and staff?		

Name of Location	Yes/No	Comments
If the organisation needs deliveries of goods, can this be done easily?		
Is the office easy to find?		
Are the office surroundings pleasant?		
Is the office itself pleasant?		
Is the office expensive?		
If the location is new for the organisation, will it be easy to equip?		
Is the office open-plan? Or are there a series of small offices?		
Is the office very noisy?		
Is there hot-desking*?		
Are there refreshment facilities for staff and/or visitors?		
Is the office near shops and restaurants? (Hint: think which category of people in the office might desire this?)		
How do staff in the building try to communicate with each other? (E.g. use emails, phone or walk to the other person's desk)		
Are there entry codes for entering the building, or for entering particular offices?		
Are the offices clearly labelled with staff member's names and departments?		
Are there an adequate number of phones?		
Are there separate offices for senior staff?		
Has the firm tried to have security of property by engraving computers and other equipment with the name of the organisation or using smart water?		
Are lockers provided for safety of personal items?		

*(This means that desks are not allocated to individuals for the whole day but are available on a 'first come first served' basis.)

Module B3 Reception Office

B3.10 Role of the reception office

Many organisations have a reception office. If you have been to a large school or college you will understand some of the roles which a reception office has. Often organisations have reception offices with similar purposes. It is important that the reception office is easy to find and if at all possible accessible to people who are physically disabled.

The reception office should be able to tell any authorised visitors where they need to go and if necessary find a suitable escort for them. This can arise if there is confidential information in the offices or if there are safety risks. Snatch thieves have been known to go into offices. People posing as workmen have been able to take many items from offices. Sometimes schools have given lanyards to authorised visitors or often visitors have a card or badge which is given to them by the receptionist and returned after the visit. They may also be given a card so that their car can be parked in the appropriate space.

If there are likely to be visitors from other countries it is helpful if the reception office has people who can speak more than one language. Sometimes there is a separate room for visitors so that confidential conversations with members of the staff can take place. This is often near the reception office which avoids people getting lost and also increases security.

The reception office may also receive mail and other deliveries or there may be a separate office for this. Some organisations will also use the reception office as a place where telephone enquires come through to and the receptionists should have a good knowledge of the organisation to be able to transfer phone calls to the right person or section.

It is important since wrong phone numbers still occur, that the receptionist gives the name of the organisation and the department, if relevant, rather than just saying "hello".

B3.20 The virtual office (instead of reception)

Rather than having a reception office, some organisations have had a virtual office which means either that the landlord of the office complex will take phone calls for an agreed sum which leaves the organisation free to do other tasks or sometimes it can be an outside body entirely where the calls are transferred at times when the main people in the organisation are not free to take phone calls.

<u>*B3.30 Project on the effectiveness of the reception office*</u>
Keep a record of the phone calls which you make to organisations. How quickly is your enquiry dealt with?

Do you have to spend a long while going through an automated system where they ask you to push "1 for new enquiries, 2 to pay bills, 3 for any problems arising from the bills, 4 for sales enquiries and 5 for orders?"

Do you then find that you have been transferred to the wrong person?

How easy is it to find the right person for the queries that you have when you visit an organisation?

From your observations can you suggest what qualities you think a receptionist should have?

Module B4 Telecommunications

B4.10 Number of phones

Most offices have a number of phones in spite of the increased use of emails. Some organisations have phones at all desks for individuals, but hot-desking has reduced the number of phones for some organisations. (Hot-desking means that staff are not guaranteed their own desk and seat during the day, and after a specified period such as one and a half hours they cannot guarantee that they will be given the same place.)

B4.20 Advantages and Disadvantages

Whilst phones are a useful method of communication they can be a distraction if people speak very loudly which means that it is difficult for other people to work. Additionally, unanswered phones can be irritating for people trying to concentrate on their work. Traditionally, one of the problems of the phone system has been that there have been no written records of conversations. This can cause problems when matters go wrong e.g. having delivery of goods being sent to the wrong place. Some organisations therefore say that they record all phone calls for training and security purposes but other people may resent this loss of privacy. Staff should be encouraged to answer telephones helpfully, for example by saying "Miss Jones, Learning Through Cooperation Limited". It is unhelpful if people just say "Hello" when you are not sure whether you have got through to the right organisation in the first place or to the right extension within an organisation. Many people resent the use of 0845 numbers which mean that the caller is paying for these, especially when they are checking on the mistakes of the organisation to which they are calling.

There are regular surveys of banks that highlight which ones have a poor track record of satisfaction. Surveys suggest that the problem of trying to contact an organisation by phone is one of the major faults identified and in fewer cases organisations contacting individuals has also been a source of complaint.

When making phone calls to businesses it is worthwhile analysing afterwards whether the business you phoned had been effective and efficient and in what ways you think that their phone policy could be improved. Some organisations use call-centre staff. Sometimes organisations use call centres in India or China, but not everyone approves of this. Some organisations will ask whether the person being telephoned is happy being called by their forename rather than by their surname. It is important if someone gives their name to make a note of it and also the organisation (if any) to which they belong. In recent years there have been problems about phone hacking mainly of people who have become famous for whatever reason. It is difficult to guard against phone hacking for people who have information which might be commercially confidential e.g. knowledge of price changes so It is worthwhile ensuring that care is taken on the phone. The usual rule is not to say anything which you would not wish to make public. There are also phone scams, particularly about deliveries of goods when the people ask about a package and are told to phone a premium rate phone line, typically over £1 per minute to get a parcel delivered. Staff can spend a long while making private phone calls during work time and, apart from the direct expense of the phone calls, it is costing the organisation money for the time which they are taking during working hours. Some general practices (GPs), hospitals and dentists now phone patients to remind them of their appointments in order to reduce the number of missed appointments, which are a huge waste of resources. Some tradespeople also confirm appointments to ensure the client is ready for them.

B4.30 Knowledge of local phone codes
It is worthwhile knowing local codes especially if your organisation receives phone calls from local people who may well be willing to place orders as well as from many potential marketing people who are unlikely to place any orders with the organisation.

B4.40 The Phone system itself
Many telephones have an automatic redialling process which reduces the possibility of dialling wrong numbers. Similarly, in many cases phone numbers which are frequently used can be inserted into the memory, it can however lead to problems if people mistakenly press the wrong button. Call display means that you can see the number and sometimes the name of the person who is calling which may be helpful to avoid nuisance calls and also helps to ensure that important phone calls are dealt with. People can have a call waiting system which means that the person being phoned knows that someone else is waiting to phone them and also tell the person who is phoning that they can leave a message. Some organisations have a direct line to certain individuals which is more helpful than having to go through a switchboard.

It is also possible to pick up phone messages from a remote point which can be helpful for salesmen and others working away from the office. It is also possible to have a call transferring system which means, particularly for small organisations, that people can still be contacted even if they are away from the main office.

B4.50 Phone packages
With many phone packages there can be a pre-paid system so that all landlines phone calls to numbers beginning with 01 (the standard phone number in the UK for most destinations outside London) and 02 which applies to the London area.

Phone calls to overseas destinations can still be very expensive in many cases, therefore the organisation for which you are working will give advice about making such calls. Even if it does not, then it is worthwhile thinking about how the phone call can be made in the most efficient manner. This may mean making notes of the main points that you wish to make and also listening carefully to any unfamiliar words or phrases. It may be worthwhile knowing the phonetic code for spelling unusual words or names.

A	Alpha
B	Bravo
C	Charlie
D	Delta
E	Echo
F	Foxtrot
G	Golf
H	Hotel
I	India
J	Juliet
K	Kilo
L	Lima
M	Mike
N	November
O	Oscar
P	Papa
Q	Quebec
R	Romeo
S	Sierra
T	Tango
U	Uniform
V	Victor
W	Whisky
X	X-ray
Y	Yankee
Z	Zulu

B4.60 Project on Telecommunications

If you are working for an organisation or for yourself, if possible make a note of the regular and non-regular people who phone you whilst working.

- *What do you notice about the efficiency of their phone calls?*
- *Are they too chatty, or do they give insufficient or imprecise information?*
- *If they use unusual names whether of people or of brands of goods and services, do they spell these out to you, perhaps using the phonetic code shown above?*
- *Is the speed at which they talk helpful, or is it too fast?*
- *If salesmen or others speak too fast, do they slow down when you ask them to or do they repeat words if you ask them?*
- *Do they speak plainly or do they slur their words?*

Using this information, write a report which suggests how organisations could improve their use of the telephone. If you are currently employed, can you think of any ways that your organisation could make better use of the telephone?

Module B5 Mail

B5.10 Inward Mail

The term inward mail is used for mail received by an organisation. In spite of emails, inward mail is still important to many organisations and will have procedures about letters which contain cheques or other valuables and there may be a register kept of these. When dealing with high value orders some will keep a record of when the letters have been received and to whom they have been forwarded. In the NHS and other organisations it may be important to keep records of any appointments which have been made.

Some organisations have a system of collecting their mail through a post office box, partly because they wish to have a prestige address. Letters which are marked confidential or private may be handled separately by the post department.

B5.20 Outgoing Mail

For outgoing mail, firms may separate first and second class mail as well as overseas mail. Some firms use franking machines which means that a record is kept of the postage.

Postal rates in the UK have risen sharply and firms may try to minimise their postage cost by printing letters on both sides of a page. Some firms also use bulk mailing which helps to reduce costs.

When sending mail, many firms have headed note paper which will show the names of directors and will also often be used as a form of publicity, possibly with a logo which sets out an idea of what the firm does.

B5.30 Project on Mail
Keep a record of any business communications sent to you.

- *What do you notice about the amount of what is called 'junk mail'? In November 2012 there were press reports saying that junk mail was about ½ of all the mail sent. Is your percentage around this?*
- *How much of the mail is directed sensibly to you e.g. does it relate to younger people, or are there details of cruises for the middle aged?*
- *What percentage of it is from charities?*

- *Do you find that some of the material is trying to persuade you to sell items, such as gold or jewellery?*
- *Is some of it from local firms such as takeaways?*

Show the information in the form of a pie chart, using Excel or any other appropriate computer program.

Module B6 Private sector organisations

B6.10 Sole traders

The term sole trader refers to the type of ownership of a business. It also means that in the event of bankruptcy there is unlimited liability which means that the owner's assets, including property, could be sold if the organisation is declared bankrupt.

In spite of all the large companies and other large organisations in the United Kingdom and elsewhere there are large numbers of sole traders. You can often recognise these organisations since they will not have company, PLC or Ltd after their name. Many corner shops and newsagents are still run as sole traders.

One of the problems which sole traders often have is taking holidays and this is another clue about whether businesses are sole traders or not since large businesses will usually remain open and will not be closed during the summer holiday season .

One of the reasons why there are still many sole traders is that it is the easiest form of business to set up. There are a minimum number of rules which have to be observed apart from health and safety ones.

Apart from the retail trade, sole traders are often found in catering, hairdressing, building repairs and maintenance, and taxi industries.

B6.20 Project on catering
This could preferably be done as a group project but can be done on your own if necessary.

Try to go to a large football club and notice that outside the football club are several small fast food vans which cater for the fans who are queuing outside.

You buy some of the food and think that there is a market for tasty, inexpensive food. You would need to check how much such a van would cost to rent or lease for a period. You would also need to check what the typical purchases are and how much it would cost to buy the necessary ingredients and how you could cook them in a confined space.

Explain how you could publicise your van e.g. by giving out leaflets containing a discount voucher to be handed in when you purchase some food., Since there are only a limited number of football matches during the course of a year are there any other events which you might be able to go to. You need to think where there are a reasonable number of people for example would it be worthwhile considering going to school or college fêtes?

David Spurling

B6.30 Partnerships
This is where two or more people agree to come together to form a partnership. The 1890 Partnership Act sets out a model partnership which is still widely adapted. There is still unlimited liability.

Partnerships give more scope for specialisation and also scope for more money to be put into the business. In some businesses one partner may know more about marketing whilst another one might know more about the technical aspects.

B6.40 Private companies and public limited companies
These types of organisations are governed by the relevant company legislation which in the United Kingdom are the 1985 & 2006 Companies Acts.

Private companies issue shares which mean that the shareholders own the business and share in the profits which are distributed as dividends according to the number of shares which they own.

There are a maximum number of 50 private shareholders within a private company.

In the United Kingdom there are also public companies where there is no limit on the number of shareholders.

B6.50 Franchises
A franchise is a licence to use the name and sell the products of another business. There are many examples of franchisors especially in the fast food sector including Burger King, Wimpy and the Body Shop.

A good franchise has the advantage that the name is well known so that it is much easier to market goods or services than for a new organisation.

B6.60 Project on Franchises
Look at some of the examples of franchises either using the above named ones or from other examples which can be obtained from websites.

- _What do you notice about the types of businesses which they are in? Many are in the fast food industry and there are also many in the cleaning industry._
- _What would be the advantages of these compared with trying to start up businesses in other ways?_

B6.70 Workers' cooperatives
The best-known workers' cooperative is the John Lewis partnership which also includes Waitrose supermarkets.

The point with workers co-operatives is that because they are owned by the workers, decisions are taken in the interest of the workers rather than solely in the interest of the directors.

B6.80 Consumers' cooperatives
These are well-known in the United Kingdom and Co-operative shops can be found in most towns and cities in the United Kingdom.

48

The Cooperative shops are owned by their members and people have to pay a small sum currently one pound to join the biggest Co-operative society. Dividends are paid at the end of a period which means that the prices are slightly cheaper than the price paid at the till.

Apart from the retail outlets there is also a Co-operative bank.

B6.90 Project on Cooperative shops
Go into a Cooperative shop and see in what ways it is similar to the other supermarkets and in what ways it differs.

- *It claims that because it is owned by its members it has different policies to the other supermarkets.*
- *In what ways does this show up e.g. are there more fair trade labels?*
- *What percentage of the products display fair trade labels?*

B6.100 Project on Cooperative banks
Either by going into a branch of the Co-operative bank or if this is not possible by looking at their website what does it claim about its lending policy and are there any particular types businesses that it will not lend money to?

- *Why does it say this?*
- *From its advertising on television or elsewhere explain how it tries to differentiate itself from the other banks?*
- *What to do you notice about the number of branches of the Co-operative bank compared with its High Street rivals?*

B6.110 Non-profit-making private sector organisations
These include building societies and mutual insurance companies. Whilst many former building societies became banks there are still a great number of building societies which means that they are owned by their customers. The Nationwide Building Society is the largest one.

B6.120 Project on types of organisations
Ideally this would be done as group project but if necessary do it on your own.

- *Look at your nearest convenient high street and if possible find out which businesses are examples of the different types of organisation. In the case of companies, somewhere on the site there should be a note of who owns the organisation and its registered office. In some cases this is going to be quite clear anyway since the high street banks will be public limited companies except for the Co-operative bank.*
- *What are the advantages and disadvantages of these organisations from the point of view of the workers and also from the point of view of the customers?*

B6.130 Project on Triodos Bank
Triodos claim that they only lend on ethical grounds. Look at their website if possible and see what they claim. Then keep press cuttings etc on the banks, especially where they are fined for different practices. Why therefore, might some people prefer to bank with Triodos rather than with some of the other banks?

Module B7 Business Risks

B7.10 Risk takers
Businesses, whether in the private or public sector, take risks. In the private sector people sometimes refer to the entrepreneur who is the businessman or woman who set up a business.

B7.20 Project on looking at a market
If you can, watch a programme such as Dragon's Den and see the ideas which arise during the course of this.

- *How do the people involved try to persuade the others that there is a market for the product which they are selling?*
- *Try to take the ideas further for example how would you know or what research you would need to do to establish whether there is such a market?*

B7.30 Insurance
Some risks can be insured against, for example firms can insure against theft of property. They can also insure against theft and fraud committed by their employees; this is called Fidelity guarantee insurance.

In some cases firms have no choice about insurance. For example every employer has to have employers' liability insurance.

Firms will also have to take out public liability insurance; even the smallest organisation may be required to take out insurance against members of the public suffering illness or injury as a result of the firm's negligence.

Motor vehicle insurance is important to any firm with its own vehicles, whether it is a local plumber with a van or a major road haulage company with a fleet of vehicles.

B7.40 Project on Honesty of Employees

- *How can firms try to ensure that their employees are honest before recruiting them?*
- *What would you do in terms of checks and might it differ between different organisations, for example if you were a farmer employing fruit pickers in the summer compared with a High Street jeweller?*

B7.50 Project on Vehicle Insurance

Using either the websites on vehicle insurance or preferably by asking firms who own their own vehicles, find out the costs of providing vehicle insurance and also what steps firms can take to minimise this cost. Some firms have an excess clause. Tabulate the information if possible in Excel or a similar program. Would this help you to choose the insurance?

There is no choice about third party insurance. Why do many people choose to have comprehensive insurance?

Module B8 Growth of organisations

B8.10 Internal and External Expansion
Firms can either expand internally through selling more goods and services or in some cases they may take over or merge with other organisations. This is called external expansion.

Takeovers can be controversial for example there was considerable controversy when Rowntree was taken over by Nestlé in 1988. Mergers take place when the owners of two different companies agree on this form of organisation.

B8.20 Project on Takeovers
If possible make a note of the controversial takeovers or mergers which take place during the course of your studies.

Which of the different stakeholders e.g. employees and shareholders, managers, customers, suppliers, trade unions, local authorities or government have different points of view about the desirability or otherwise of these takeovers or mergers and why?

B8.30 Vertical integration backwards and forwards
Vertical integration occurs when firms take over their suppliers in which case it is called vertical integration backwards. This might occur for example if a firm wishes to have control over its food supply or it can be vertical forward if it takes over firms which it is supplying.

Many breweries for example have taken over public houses which are called tied pubs.

We similarly find that many of the petrol companies also own garages and the petrol pumps which is another example of vertical integration.

B8.40 Lateral integration
In some cases there can be lateral integration which is also sometimes known by the term conglomerates whereby firms in different industries form part of a larger one. One of the largest examples of lateral integration is Unilever. It includes detergents, soap, and ice cream amongst many other products.

B8.50 Reasons for organisations wishing to grow
There are a number of different reasons why firms might wish to grow, in some cases there may be little choice if a firm wants to have technical economies of scale. In the oil tanker business,

operating a larger 500,000 tonne supertanker by no means costs 10 times a 50,000 tonne tanker, and the number of crew is reasonably similar whatever the size of the tanker.

B8.60 Project on Road Haulage vehicles
Find out the costs of road haulage vehicles of different sizes ranging from small vans to the largest road haulage vehicles.

Plot on a suitable graph the size and cost and then calculate using Excel if possible or a similar computer program, the cost per tonne capacity.

What you notice about the shape of the graph?

Why do road haulage firms not always use the largest possible lorries?

B8.70 Managerial economies
The cost of a manager will often be the same even if they are supervising more employees.

In other cases the cost of setting up a computer will not vary proportionately according to the number of people using it or the amount it is used, so it will be proportionately cheaper to manage a larger system.

There is also greater scope for job specialisation with a larger organisation.

B8.80 Project on Large and Small Firms
Compare and contrast a small organisation for example a local shop, taxi firm or building contractor with a larger organisation.

- *What do you notice about the tasks people do in the larger organisation?*

- *Are they more specialised?*

- *Does the larger firm or organisation use more capital equipment proportionately?*

B8.90 Diseconomies of scale
Whilst there has been great emphasis on even larger organisations, many people feel that this may have gone too far. In particular they have pointed to the example of the banks and other financial institutions where there have been many scandals about the ways that these organisations have acted. It surprised some people that an individual could be accused of wrongly handling £1.8 billion of money without adequate safeguards in UBS (a major Swiss bank).

There are several main reasons why these diseconomies arise. The first is that the chain of command can become too long. (This refers to the number of layers in the organisation.)Messages which are meant to be passed up the chain frequently do not reach the top. The second is that too many people have to pass their information to one person. This is called the span of control.

B8.100 Project on Organisation charts
Preferably do this in a group but if this is not possible do this as an individual.

If you are working show, using an organisation chart if possible, the number of layers in the organisation and the span of control.

How well do the communications work from the top downwards and also from the bottom upwards?

If you are not currently employed carry out the same tasks but looking at a school or college of which you have knowledge.

Module B9 Production methods

There are a variety of methods of production.

B9.10 Unit production

One of these methods is called unit production; sometimes it is called one off production. This can apply to items such as wedding cakes, to designer clothes where people want their clothes to be individually made to measure, or to houses where usually richer people will have their own architect to design a house which is different to those around it.

Usually unit production is labour-intensive which means that more labour is used than in other forms of production.

B9.20 Batch production

Batch production occurs when the products are made in batches for example in some cases the furnace will limit the number of items which can be made at any one stage. Similarly in a baker, the number of loaves or cakes that can be made may be limited by the size of the oven.

B9.30 Mass production

Mass production is more common nowadays and is clearly seen in the car market. It lends itself very much to automation or even to use of robots in some cases. Robots have the advantage that they do not get tired and can be used in places where people do not wish to work. They can also be used for spraying paint or chemicals.

Mass production is also now used in conditions which would not have been thought of in the past, for example with railway station buildings which can be largely prefabricated. This means that the station buildings are not constructed on site, but elsewhere and then transported to the station.

B9.40 Flow Production

This applies to products such as oil or water where the capacity is determined by the size of the pipelines.

B9.50 Project on Mass Production

If you know of people who are working in mass production and they are willing to be interviewed then ask them what are the advantages and disadvantages of working in such an environment.

In many cases with mass production there is shift work so that the expensive machines etc can be used very extensively. Why might it be difficult to get workers to work the night shift?

If you cannot find people to interview directly then do the project indirectly by imagining under what circumstances you would be willing to work different shifts and what the advantages and disadvantages would be.

Some firms employ workers on a perpetual night shift whilst in other cases there is rotation so that people may work on the night shift one week in three. Explain clearly why organisations might wish to use either method.

Firms have sometimes used job rotation so that people do more than one job. Sometimes they do this to minimise boredom and sometimes they do this so that if workers for whatever reason are not available then other people can carry on doing the work.

Explain why you think that some would like to have job rotation whilst other people might not wish to do so.

Firms have also sometimes used job enlargement so that workers can carry out more tasks rather than fewer. Why might some people prefer to do this?

Module B10 The Human Relations Department

B10.10 Wages and Salaries

Wages and salaries are in many organisations the largest single item of expenditure. Even apart from this, staff are important since in most cases the difference between an efficient and inefficient organisation will be the quality of staff and how they are used. You will have discovered this from schools and colleges which you know. We can see some schools and colleges which are well equipped but do not provide such a good standard of organisation as other schools and colleges with similar students but better staff.

B10.20 Queues

Whilst the British have a reputation for enjoying queues, people get irritated if they have to join a long queue for no obvious reason. This applies when it is a physical queue at an airport in bad weather or at a supermarket checkout. Even worse is when you are paying for a phone call and the company says "We have an unusually high volume of calls" and every time you try to reach them this message occurs at whatever time of day. An efficient organisation will try to reduce the length of time people are waiting in phone queues by having more staff. An efficient retailer is likely to try to reduce the length of queues by getting staff to take over if there are empty tills. Whilst firms often have notices saying that "Staff should not be harassed" it would often be better if the underlying causes of stress to both staff and customers or clients could be reduced in the first place.

B10.30 The Workplace

Adequate heating is prescribed by UK law, but even where it is not it is sensible to have offices which are neither too warm nor too cold. Excessive heat will cause drowsiness. A firm which has considerable litter outside or even worse inside its buildings will give a bad impression.

B10.40 Project on efficiency

Explain how most people judge efficiency or inefficiency of the organisation from the staff that they contact.

Explain this in terms of any phone conversations, the amount of time taken to answer phone calls, the pleasantness and efficiency of staff especially if things go wrong.

Explain what else gives the impression of efficiency for example if you are waiting in a queue for a long while with no obvious reason for this delay.

B10.50 Project on annual reports
If you look at a company's annual report you will see that it gives a lot of data about the number of employees as well as, in some cases, their productivity. What do you notice about the number of employees over a period?

Try to explain the trends.

B10.60 Recruitment

Staff may be recruited by advertisements in the local or national press, through websites or through word-of-mouth, for example asking people within the organisation if they know anybody who would be suitable. Job centres can be used by organisations wishing to recruit staff. Specialist agencies are sometimes used for recruitment. This can apply to secretarial staff. Sometimes for various senior posts, organisations use head-hunters whereby firms with specialist knowledge are used to recruit specialist people.

B10.70 Project on recruiting
Look at the ways that organisations try to recruit new staff.

Even if you are not currently looking for work ask your friends and/or family how they were recruited for their jobs.

Put this information in terms of a pie chart or another suitable form.

Ask them about the efficiency or otherwise of the recruiting process.

Did they feel that the interview (if they had one) was sensible and asked relevant questions?

If not how could the interview process have been improved?

Module B11 Accounting

B11.10 Purpose of Accounting

Whilst traditionally accounting was concerned with bookkeeping, which means that records were kept of both income and expenditure, the emphasis has changed to management accounting. (If you are interested in bookkeeping, the International Association of Bookkeepers has an excellent system of examinations where the fees are much lower than most other bodies.) The main purpose of accounting is to ensure that there are sufficient financial controls in any organisation.

Firms in the private sector will usually aim at profitability looking both at income which is sometimes called revenue as well as expenses.

In principle this is no different from an individual who needs to look at their income and expenses over time.

Apart from internal controls there are also external controls by the auditors.

Within an organisation the accountants will want to look at different expenses which have occurred and whether this is the best use of money and other resources.

One of the features of the internal control is to check that the businesses providing goods and services are of suitable quality. Organisations also need to check that their existing or potential customers are going to repay their debts. This has become even more important since the credit crunch problems arose from 2008 onwards in the UK and elsewhere.

An organisation will wish to show cash budgets showing both the outflows and the inflows.

B11.20 Project on Taxis

Imagine you are working for a taxi company which is about to purchase a new taxi for £15,000.

Imagine also it has typical fares for a trip averaging £5 for the trip and the firm typically makes 50 such trips in the day whilst the driver is paid £12,000 a year on a monthly basis. You might also need to assume what the costs are of fuel and oil.

You should be able to obtain information from websites or from observation at the petrol pumps etc.

Do you assume that the firm makes exactly the same number of trips everyday?

When would you expect the taxis to be busy and when would you expect them to be less busy?

Why would some firms like to have contracts for school runs even if the amount per trip is lower than if they were sitting on a taxi rank?

Set out clearly what costs a taxi firm will need to cover even if the taxi was off the road because of repairs.

Set out in a table with a column for income and a column for expenditure what costs you would expect to find in such an organisation and what revenue they would obtain.

<u>*B11.30 Project on Financial scandals*</u>
Make a note of any financial scandals which occur and if possible use either press cuttings or information from websites etc.

What does this show about the financial information which was available to customers, employees and suppliers?

If possible try to find out any information about the auditors and whether they have exercised 'due diligence'. This rather odd phrase means have they done what they reasonably should have been expected to do.

Module B12 Finance

B12.10 Importance of finance

All organisations whether in the private or public sector need money to set up and to be able to expand if necessary. When considering finance, organisations will need to consider how long they require any money for. They may need short term finance, for example, a baker might need money to buy additional quantities of flour if they are preparing for a major celebration for which they need to produce more cakes etc. Organisations will also need to consider what security they can offer. They will also need to consider any risks involved in obtaining money.

Businesses need money on a day-to-day basis which is called working capital to buy goods and services. They also need long-term capital to be able to buy capital assets such as factories, retail outlets, expensive machinery as well as vehicles.

B12.20 Methods of finance

Most small traders will start their business using personal savings. Where this is insufficient many may often borrow money from banks or building societies using their houses as security. This however has led to problems not just in the UK but in other countries when people could no longer afford the interest and capital repayments. Because of this houses are repossessed. In the private sector firms may have money from retained profits, this means money which is not given to shareholders in the form of dividends.

Firms may be able to borrow money through overdrafts or loans. Overdrafts mean that the bank allows them to borrow up to a certain amount. Interest on bank loans is paid on the whole amount of the loan although since the credit crunch in 2008, loans have become more difficult to find. Firms may also be able to lease some items such as vehicles or buy some items on hire purchase. Firms may also use trade credit for example not paying money immediately but of course this involves risk. Many firms offer a discount if money is paid within a short time, such as within seven days. Large firms may issue shares or debentures. Where the businesses are owed money they will sometimes approach firms for factoring. This means they pass on these debts for an agreed percentage to a firm which specialises in factoring.

Financial Institutions

The major financial institutions in the UK are very important. The financial institutions may include pension funds, insurance funds, banks and building societies. The financial institutions are the major shareholders of the large firms in this country.

David Spurling

The stock exchange, not just in this country, but in other countries, is also important and there has been an alternative investment market which helps other organisations. An example of this is 'Ethical Property' which specialises in refurbishing existing buildings, improves their energy efficiency and then lets them out to charities and social venture organisations.

B12.30 Project on finance
Using information from the internet or the financial press, fill in the table below showing the typical interest rates at the time when you complete it.

Type of finance	Lowest rate available	Security required (if any) and comments
Interest rate on authorised overdraft		
Interest rate on unauthorised overdraft		
Interest rate on bank Loans		
Interest rate on mortgages		
Interest rate on store cards		
Interest rate on credit cards		
Interest rate from pawnbrokers		

B12.40 Project on setting up a nightclub
You decide that there is a market for dances with a particular type of music which is not catered for locally. Many young people you know have commented about this.

Explain what finance you might need in order to be able to have suitable premises in the short run.

Explain where you could obtain this.

Explain where you could obtain the money for your own premises which would give you the advantage of security.

What money is required for?	Type of finance you would consider	Costs of finance	Time taken to obtain this (often called opportunity cost of time)
Short term finance			
Printing of tickets			
Hiring of hall			
Loudspeakers			
Security guards/bouncers			
Publicity (e.g. leaflets, local radio)			
Fill in more items here...			
Long term finance			
Leasing or purchase of suitable venue			
Equipment at venue			
Insurance costs			
Maintenance costs			

B12.50 Public Sector

In the public sector money is found through general taxation such as income tax, VAT, National Insurance and corporation tax. Corporation tax is a tax on company profits. The government may also borrow money.

The local authorities get some money from council tax. This is a tax on all properties in England which is levied by the local council. In counties such as Kent a local borough council (e.g. Swale Borough Council) receives the money although the majority of expenditure goes to Kent County Council.

B12.60 Project on central government
Using current data from economic trends or other websites complete the following table.

We have started to complete some comments in the third column, but you should be able to find much more information from either the financial press or from websites etc.

Government revenue

Type of revenue	Amount raised	Comments
Income tax		*Look for example at income tax thresholds as well as standard rate of tax.*
National Insurance		
Corporation tax		
Taxation on expenditure		
Inheritance tax		

Type of revenue	Amount raised	Comments
Value added tax (VAT)		
Vehicle excise duty (Often called road tax)		
Other taxes		

B12.70 Project on local authorities
Find out what your local authority area is and almost certainly they will have a website which shows where they get their money from and what they spend it on.

Plot this data in a suitable form e.g. pie chart etc.

Explain what difficulties your local authority is currently facing and how it intends to resolve any problems e.g. sale of certain assets or reduction in certain services.

B12.80 Case Study on a road haulage business
A road haulage business is located near a busy main road which was originally much quieter. When the depot was started it was near the owner's house and there were few other houses around.

The area has subsequently become much more built up and the neighbours frequently complain about the lorries in terms of safety and noise although they knew that the depot was there when they bought their houses.

Explain what the road haulage firm could do and how it could find the money to have a new purpose built depot in another area.

Q1 What would you expect to find about land prices in the centre of the town?

Q2 What would you expect to find about land prices in the industrial estates? (An industrial estate is the name given to the buildings often used by small firms and others for manufacturing plastics, parcel firms, light engineering etc.)

Q3 Why in most towns and cities is industry kept separate from housing?

Module B13 Purchasing

B13.10 Reasons for purchasing

Organisations whether in the private or the public sector have to make purchases. The purchasing department is an important one in manufacturing where they will usually keep a list of potential suppliers as well as the existing ones. This applies whether it is purchasing raw materials, machinery, computers or food and drink (if the organisation has canteen or restaurant facilities).

The public sector would also need purchasing officers and with government cutbacks there has been more emphasis on joint purchasing by fire brigades, police, and the NHS.

Local authorities have also been encouraged to make joint purchases particularly of computers and related software.

B13.20 Project on your own purchases
Make a list of the purchases which you make during the course of a time period such as a month.

How do you decide on the major purchases for example do you look around a variety of sources or do you simply go to the ones you already know?

Using this approach then consider how you would try to purchase major items such as computers, printers, stationery, vehicles, if you were working for a large manufacturer.

Explain what information you would require about prices and after sales service if relevant as for example with vehicles and computer equipment.

Would you want to keep to one supplier?

Many organisations insist on getting at least three quotations for any major purchase. Some other organisations however suggest that they would rather keep to one organisation if possible since they then get a better service. With rises in fuel prices, organisations have sometimes looked to see whether they could reduce their fuel consumption, rather than merely switching suppliers.

How could any organisations of which you have knowledge try to reduce their fuel bills without affecting the organisation in a negative way?

From your own knowledge of personal purchases explain the merits and disadvantages of both approaches.

B13.30 Stock control

Organisations need stocks especially where demand is uncertain. Firms need to consider the costs of what would happen if they do not have adequate stocks against the risks of having too much stock. If they have too much stock, particularly with perishable items, they will have problems if they are left with unsellable stock. This may also apply to what is sometimes called commercially perishable stock, such as today's newspapers, CD's or fashionable clothes. If, on the other hand, you go to a shop and frequently they do not have what you require, then you may well turn to alternatives.

B13.40 Project on ice-cream vans

Think of a simple organisation such as an ice-cream van vendor.

Look at the prices if you have a local van and see what they charge.

Compare these prices with the charges which are made in the local shop and plot these figures using Excel or a similar computer program if possible.

What will happen if the ice-cream van runs out of stock especially in a remote area?

What will happen on the other hand if the van has stock which it cannot use?

Module B14 Marketing

14.10 The importance of marketing.

Marketing is something we are all aware of. Every night you will see adverts on the commercial channels on television. Typically people watch about twenty hours of television per week. You can find out from government websites the maximum amount of advertising per hour. Marketing however is not just advertising, but can involve market research as well as promotion and advertising. Product placement is now allowed which means that organisations are allowed to show a particular brand in a television program. Therefore, in a show they can see a particular brand of watch, phone, food etc. In televised football matches the audience can clearly see billboards showing the name of brands of products. If there are bans on advertising some products such as cigarettes or alcohol, having the names of these products on sports shirts or racing cars may be a way of getting round this. Often if a football match is between two foreign sides but the audience is likely to be British, there will be advertisements geared to the British TV audience rather than to the spectators. The word 'subliminal' is sometimes used to mean advertising which is not noticed directly but which the brain absorbs subconsciously.

14.20 Marketing segments (young people)

Many banks try to attract young customers since they assume that bank customers are often loyal and once they have gained one they will not transfer elsewhere.

How do they try to attract young people in the first place? Sometimes they may give a free rail card or say that they will not charge overdraft fees in the first few months. A great deal of advertising will try to appeal to young people, for example with brightly coloured sweets to attract the very young.

14.30 Marketing segments (older people)

Older people may need chairlifts and they may carry out market research to see if someone has a disability and then make an appointment to see them if they have. They may also advertise housing for the elderly in suitable magazines.

14.40 The 4 P's (Product, Price, Place and Promotion)

Sometimes the **product** may arise as a by-product of what organisations are trying to do. For example, the mouse is frequently used on computers and the computer manufacturers wished to get people to be able to use this efficiently. Computer games were one way of getting many people to use the mouse and to enjoy themselves at the same time. Computer games now rely heavily on finding out what young people in particular want and then catering for this market.

Psychological pricing is often used e.g. the **price** will be £999.95 .The phrase 'elastic and inelastic' is often used by economists and marketing staff. An inelastic demand is one which does not vary much according to price. For example, demand for petrol for journeys to and from work will not vary even if the price rises considerably. On the other hand, if there are close substitutes as with some brands of petrol, people would transfer from one brand to another if the price of one rose but the others did not.

Place can be important. Many shops find that the footfall is much greater if they are located in the centre of a high street than in a side street. Similarly, an ice cream salesman is much more likely to find a market at a football match in the summer or at a seaside resort than in many other places.

Promotion is important and financial institutions have sponsored sporting events in order to get their name better known.

14.50 After sales service
Many people are concerned that if they buy an expensive product and it goes wrong that repairs may mean they are faced with a heavy expense and also that they will not be able to use the product. Several shops now advertise that their guarantees are longer lasting than their rivals.

14.60 Persuasive advertising used by government
Whilst we usually think of marketing as selling a good or service there are some goods such as harmful drugs which governments are trying to limit the sales on. They may use slogans like "drugs can make you ugly" to counteract the glamorous image which people have of drugs. Sometimes they are trying to persuade people to have more educational training. They may use websites or sometimes visits to schools to sell these.

Self-examination questions
Q1. What do you notice about advertising on television?

Make a note of how much relevant information is given and also what it leaves out.

Hint: If you were buying a car, what are the most important things you need to know?

Does the advertisement tell you this?

Q2. Make a note of the amount of commercial television you watch in a week. If possible, ask a group of friends to do the same.

How much of this time is taken up by advertisements?
Make a pie chart of what type of products are being advertised e.g. cars, detergents, etc.
What do you notice about the different times of day and different products being advertised? What might this tell you about market segmentation?

Q3. Many people regard personal finance as a rather boring subject whether it is insurance or bank accounts. How can the financial institutions try to get themselves better known?

Will sponsorship of sporting events help to overcome the problems of name recognition?

Q4. There are several different segments in the footwear market.

How do firms try to sell functional footwear e.g. boots for walking outdoors?

How does this compare with trying to sell designer label shoes?

Q5. It is often said that past customers are the best salesmen since people recommend products and services by word of mouth.

Is this true of all goods and services and how can an organisation which gives a good service try to take advantage of this?

Q6. If you have had to choose a school or college, what factors have influenced you?

Will a glossy brochure, TV advertisement or newspaper article have made a good impression on you?

Q7. Some organisations have taken part in competitions to show that they are the best employers in their area.

Why might this be an effective way of publicising their organisation?

Q8. A number of organisations use well-known people such as sports and TV personalities to advertise their products. This was especially true around the time of the London 2012 Olympics.

Why do people take notice of these advertisements?

Q9. How can a school or college which wishes to raise funds ensure that it publicises a dance in a cost effective way?

Q10. How can the railways try to get younger people to travel with them?

Q11. If a distance learning college wishes to persuade more people to take their courses, how can it do this?

Q12. The present government wants more people to take up apprenticeships. How can it persuade young people to do this? What do you notice about the ways that they try to use websites?

Q13. Make a note of any advertisements which mention guarantees.

What products are these trying to sell and why might guarantees be important?

What is the cost of these guarantees, if any?

Q14. How could a small environmental organisation which specialises in providing solar panels and heat extractors try to market their products?

Module B15 Distribution of goods

B15.10 What is distribution?
Distribution means how goods get from the supplier (for example farmers or oil producers which are part of what is called primary production) to the final customer.

If we take a simple example with one product we show below some of the stages in the production process and distribution which are necessary to get the goods from one place to another.

Table 1

Type of Production	Occupation	Goods being distributed
Primary production	Farmer	Wheat
Secondary production	Miller	Loaves
Tertiary production	Wholesaler	Loaves in a different place
Tertiary production	Lorry drivers	Loaves in a different place
Tertiary production	Retailers	Loaves in a different place
Tertiary production	Customers sometimes known as consumers	Loaves in a different place

B15.20 Project on loaves
Expand the ideas in table 1 to show in a flow diagram what other processes would be involved.

In this example if the lorry is using diesel how would this have got to the lorry in the first place?

B15.30 Supply Chains
Traditionally there was often a supply chain which went from the manufacturers to the wholesalers who bought in bulk, stored products and in many cases advertised the product.

In turn these went to the retailer sometimes to small shops and sometimes to the voluntary chains as well as to the large supermarkets.

B15.40 Online shopping
There is a revolution going on at the present time with the retail trade with many people now using online shopping so that in effect the shops come to the people rather than people going to the shops.

B15.50 The importance of distribution

Distribution is a large and important part of the total economy. There are a large number of costs involved such as packaging and costs of insurance.

Fuel costs are likely to rise in the future so it is important that lorries are both well maintained and that the drivers know where they are going and if possible can have their deliveries arranged so that they minimise the cost to the organisation. Whilst lorries are used extensively, the present government is trying to increase the volume of traffic going by rail and greater use of the Channel Tunnel will help.

B15.60 Project on the high street
Look at a High street which is near to you.

Show on a bar chart or pie chart or any suitable diagram which are the different types of retailers located in the high street.

Referring to the different types of retailers, explain in a few sentences which of these would seem to be vulnerable to online shopping and which might be less vulnerable giving your reasons.

Are there any other types of business which might be able to flourish in your high street?

For example are there any leisure activities which people of your age group or other age groups are not catered for?

B15.70 Project on electrical goods
Look at the goods in a typical electrical department or electrical store.

Which countries do most of the items come from?

What methods of transport do you think firms would have used in order to get the items to the shops?

B15.80 Containers

Containers are a large box which has traditionally been 8 foot by 8 foot (2.438m) by a multiple of 10 foot (3.048m). Because they have been this standard size it has been easy to transfer them from road to rail or ship and vice versa. Recently large containers have been 9ft 6 inches (2.826m) high which has posed problems for the railway but some of the railway system has been adapted to cater for this height.

B15.90 Project on containers
If you are travelling as a car passenger especially on the motorways make a note of the number of containers which you see which are easily recognisable.

You will usually be able to tell whether they are from the United Kingdom or from overseas by the registration number.

What proportion is from overseas? In some cases you should be able to see what regular routes they run.

What do you notice about these?

Module B16 Organisation and methods (O&M)

B16.10 What is O and M?

O&M look for the quickest, cheapest ways of providing good quality outputs. This can apply to manufacturing of goods to the right specification. It can also be applied to service industries so that the right number of people are employed at the right time and place.

Sometimes this may be a separate department and sometimes it may be a section. What it means is that firms look at the different processes involved in their organisation and try to find out whether there are more efficient ways of carrying out these processes.

If we look around at almost any organisation we can see that methods are changing.

In the transport sector more emphasis is placed on buying tickets in advance for coaches, railways, shipping (including cruises) or the airlines. These may be ordered on line, by phone or at a terminal or by post.

With general practitioners (GP's), large numbers of people do not turn up for appointments which is a waste of resources so that in some cases receptionists or others may try to phone people beforehand to reduce this waste.

B16.20 Project on Doctors

If you go to a doctor's surgery what do you notice about the role of the receptionist?

Do they have an electronic signing in process and what information do patients have to give e.g. some patients have to give the date of birth?

Why you think they ask for this information? Hint: think of names which are common e.g. David Smith.

In the waiting room how are people informed when it is their turn to be seen by the doctor, nurse etc?

Do people quickly respond to this or do the nurses or doctors have to come to the waiting room?

Module B17 Sources of information

B17.10 The information age
We live in what is sometimes called the information age and as most people are aware we can obtain information from a variety of sources including websites as well as the social media. One of the problems however, is checking that what appears to be true is true rather than repeating information which is false.

B17.20 Public libraries
In spite of cutbacks, libraries are a good source of information for text books and reference books as well as allowing access to websites and e-mails.

It is worthwhile spending time checking the classification system of the library and librarians usually will give you help in this way. The Dewey system is the most common in public libraries, with different numbers for different non-fiction categories such as 330 for Economics.

If you are working in an organisation which deals with people overseas, atlases can give you an idea which places are important and where they located. Some will often give the population as well as giving you an economic profile.

B17.30 Project on Eastern Europe
Imagine that you're dealing with a business which is trying to export courses and textbooks to Eastern Europe.

What information would you require about these countries and where could you obtain it?

Make a table of the main information that you have acquired, for example languages that are spoken, and an idea of typical incomes.

Explain how you could use this information when reporting back to your boss.

B17.40 Dictionaries
Dictionaries are still an important source of information and whilst most computers have their own dictionary which can be very helpful, it is still possible to come across words which are not in these.

B17.50 Wikipedia

This is a widely used free encyclopaedia which gives sources of information on a wide variety of topics. The editors always are willing to receive more information if the topic is labelled as a stub. If you can help, then in turn this will make this an even more valuable source of information.

B17.60 Book shops

Whilst many people buy books online, the smaller independent book shops can often offer good advice on the best books to buy. In some cases, Oxfam in particular has a wide range of second-hand books which can often be very useful.

B17.70 Project on new words
Keep a note of any new words that you come across. Then look up the definitions of these words and if possible see how you could use these words in any work that you have to do.

B17.80 Project on errors
Make a note of any errors that you come across in advertising or notices. For what businesses might this be important?

B17.90 Project on Dictionaries and Thesaurus
Look at a good dictionary such as Collins Cobuild Dictionary. Explain why it might be helpful to know the different parts of speech such as nouns, verbs, adverbs and adjectives, especially if you wish to translate the words into another language. Explain as well why you might wish to use a thesaurus which can be found included in most word-processing applications.

Module B18 Business meetings

B18.10 Importance of meetings
In many organisations meetings are important. This could include what is sometimes called B2B, this stands for business to business and people attend these meetings partly because networking is thought to be important.

In most of these meetings people typically speak for 30 seconds to 1 minute. It is often difficult to remember who has said what so it is helpful to jot down a few notes of what they have said and what organisation they represent. This is particularly important if networking with these people is likely to be helpful to you or your organisation, or you can help them.

If you are attending a business meeting it is important to check where it is and how to get there. Arriving late at the meeting can obviously be embarrassing for most people and apart from this it gives a bad impression of both you and the organisation which you are representing.

B18.20 Project on success of meetings
If you go to any business meetings or other meetings, make a note of how well or otherwise you think the chairperson is doing.

Does the chairperson seem to be in control?

Do they allow people to be able to put their points across and can they keep order?

Do they on the other hand ignore some people (usually the less vocal people)?

Do they allocate time well?

Do they allow for a range of views to be put across? Some agendas try to specify time limits on particular items.

Are the people who speak from the floor well informed and do they make their points successfully?

Do people simply repeat what previous speakers have said rather than raising any new points?

Do people use acronyms which other people do not understand? (Acronyms are abbreviations of the organisation's name. Some such as BBC do not need to be explained but others may be unfamiliar to some people at the meeting.)

Do people use jargon which other people have not understood?

Are there any ways in which the meeting could have been improved?

If you are not able to go to any meetings you could watch any debates on television and make the same points.

<u>Typical Agenda</u>

Meeting of Learning Through Cooperation Ltd

Date: 11/1/2015

Item	Time	Time allocated
Chairperon's welcome and introduction of any new people	10 a.m.	10 minutes
Minutes of the last meeting and matters arising	10.10 a.m.	15 minutes
Chairperson's report and questions	10.25 a.m.	10 minutes
Treasurer's report and questions	10.35 a.m.	10 minutes
Secretary's report and questions	10.45 a.m.	15 minutes
Press officer's report and questions	11.00 a.m.	20 minutes
A.O.B *(This is the abbreviation for Any Other Business)*	11.20 a.m.	10 minutes
Close of formal business and time for informal networking including refreshments	11.30 a.m.	30 minutes

B18.30 Project on using a meeting to publicise your organisation
If you are working for an organisation imagine that you are asked to talk for 30 seconds to a minute, and that you can if necessary bring leaflets or other material which can be distributed to the other people at the meeting. Some organisations will let you publicise your organisation through a short PowerPoint presentation.

How could you use this effectively?

If you are not currently working for an organisation then think of one which you know something about.

What main points would you wish to make about your organisation

How could you give this information in the most effective way?

Module B19 Arranging visits

B19.10 Arranging travel

Clerical staff often arrange visits for their own staff and sometimes for visitors to the office. It is important if people are travelling by public transport that staff have an idea of the transport system and also the most cost effective way of getting to or from the office.

The railways have a bewildering number of fares so it is helpful to be able to find the best ones. Chester-le-Track (Tel: 01913871387) are probably the most helpful organisation if you can arrange visits more than seven days in advance, since you speak to a person. It may also be helpful particularly if people are disabled or have a lot of luggage to know about the local taxi service and where it can pick up.

If people are travelling overseas, then the Lonely Planet guides are very helpful since they try to be impartial rather than gushy.

If they are going to a country where there may be health problems then the Department of Health can give advice.

If they are going to a country where there may be political problems then it is worthwhile contacting the UK Foreign and Commonwealth office.

B19.20 Overseas visits and documentation

If the visits are overseas then it is important that people have up-to-date passports as well as Visas if necessary. These can take a while to come through and similarly if someone does not already have a passport, there can be delays in obtaining one so it is important to plan in advance.

With overseas visits it is important that the necessary currency is available or arrangements have been made by the organisation for obtaining currency whilst abroad. There are a number of websites claiming to give the best currency options.

Security checks at borders can take a while so particularly if people are travelling by air people need to allow for this.

It is also important that overseas visitors are aware of public holidays and similarly if people from the home country are visiting overseas.

Chambers of commerce including Kent Invicta Chamber of Commerce have a members' diary which shows the currency, the capital and National Holidays and also the time differences between

Greenwich meantime and other countries. This information can be helpful. Few executives or others want to receive phone calls at 3 o' clock in the morning!

B19.30 Knowledge of other cultures and languages

It is very important to be tactful when going overseas for example it is helpful to know that neither Muslims nor Jews eat meat from pigs. Therefore it would be unwise to include food containing bacon or ham at a reception. This is unlikely to endear oneself to the people concerned.

B19.40 Project on visits to emerging economies

You are asked to arrange visits for your office managers to go to one of the emerging economies as they are sometimes called for example India, China or Brazil.

What documentation would you need to consider?

Why might it be important to consider any medical conditions that the staff have and also any dietary requirements?

Why might it be important to know about any public holidays and also the typical days or hours that the staff work in another country?

Why might it be important as well to check on suitable accommodation in the country which they are visiting?

Module B20 Looking for jobs

B20.10 Training for office work

Traditionally most people working in an office did not receive formal training. The number of office workers has increased dramatically in the UK but there has been more emphasis on training in recent years. At the present time there is considerable discussion about whether people should go on to university or other higher education or whether they should look at alternative routes and qualifications.

Conventional route	Age at completion	Comment
GCSEs	16	
A-levels	18	No earnings
Degrees	21	No earnings

Less conventional route	Age at completion	Comment
GCSEs	16	Full-time education until 18
Vocational training / Apprenticeships	18	Earnings (a minimum wage is specified)
Further apprenticeships or professional training	21	Earnings (a minimum wage is specified)

There are a many other considerations which come into this choice.

For some jobs such as those in the medical profession there is little choice but to go to university. For other jobs such as those in accountancy there is a much wider choice of routes.

B20.20 Project on your career

Either from a careers office or from appropriate websites, make an appropriate table for the career of your choice.

Explain at what ages you might be able to take examinations which might be necessary for your career and what earnings you might reasonably expect to have in these periods. Also look at the cash flow during these periods.

If you know people who are either currently or have recently been at university, get an estimate of the cost of accommodation and the costs of transport to and from college.

How much they will have to pay back in tuition fees, and when, if they have satisfactory earnings and similarly see the current rates of pay for apprentices.

Using this information, write a brief report outlining the advantages and disadvantages of the different career paths/routes?

Have a look at the IAB website. What are the costs of taking their examinations compared with many others? What are the potential benefits? Could you take the examinations by distance learning, for example through Learning Through Cooperation Ltd?

B20.30 CV

Most people now have their CV on a computer and they may well alter it slightly to give the greater emphasis for the post for which they are applying. For example, someone applying to work as an assistant to a vet might stress the work they have done with animals on the school farm. Whereas if they were applying for the post of clerical assistant for a children's nursery this experience would be less relevant than the time they have spent either formally or informally in childcare.

B20.40 Example of a CV
Miss Smith
Address: 1 Smith Street, Smithtown, Smithshire, ZZ99 3CZ
Home Number: 01632 960567
Mobile Number: 07700900567
Email: smithsmith@smith.soc.uk

Profile

I am an organised, punctual, enthusiastic and adaptable person with good writing skills. During my time at school, I have been involved in drama productions, choirs, and art groups, which has provided me with an ability to work in a team effectively. I welcome a challenge, and will always work to the best of my ability. I am enthusiastic about learning new skills including voice input although my current word processing skills are good.

Education
All taken at Smith College, Smith Street, Smith town, Smithshire, ZZ99 3CZ

A Levels

English Literature – B	September 2013 – June 2015
History – B	September 2013 – June 2015
Sociology – A	September 2013 – June 2015

GCSE's

English – A	September 2011 – January 2013
English Literature – A	September 2011 – June 2013
History – A	September 2011 – June 2013
Science – B	September 2011 – June 2013
Mathematics – B	September 2011 – November 2012
Additional Science – C	September 2011 – June 2013
Music – C	September 2011 – June 2013
Religious Studies	
(Short Course) – A	September 2011 – June 2012
Religious Studies – A	September 2011 – June 2013

Edexcel Level 2 BTEC First Diploma

Art and Design – Distinction	September 2011 – June 2013

OCR Level 2 National First Award

ICT – Merit	September 2010 – June 2013

OCR Level 2 National Award

ICT – Merit	September 2010 – June 2013

AQA Level 1 and Level 2 Certificate
Preparation for

Working Life – Level 2	September 2010 – June 2011

---

o   **Interests**

From a very young age I have been interested in reading. I enjoy reading, from classics to modern day literature. This has enhanced my writing skills and allowed me to gain a wider range of vocabulary. In addition to this, I enjoy art which I have improved on since taking it as a BTEC option during my GCSE's as it has allowed me to explore a variety of new techniques. As well as this, I am experimenting in other crafts, including cross-stitching, card making and mosaics. I am also learning to play the keyboard through video tutorials on the internet, and hope to get lessons in the future.

References

Mr Brown
Head of Sociology
Smith Street
Smith Town
Smithshire
ZZ99 3CZ

Mrs Green
Head of English
Smith Street
Smith Town
Smithshire
ZZ99 3CZ

B20.50 Example Reference 1

Mr Brown
Head of A Level Sociology
Smith College

25 August 2015

REFERENCE FOR MISS CHARLOTTE SMITH

Having taught Charlotte for the last two years I am able to make the following comments concerning her capabilities and character.

First, as her A Level results show, she is an intellectually gifted individual who has a logical and systematic mind which she has applied with dedication, commitment and enthusiasm. In addition her punctuality and attendance have been excellent. In short, she has been a model student.

With regard to her character I would like to make the following points: she is a determined individual, but one who manifestly cares for the well being of others i.e. she is both sympathetic and empathic in her dealings with people - as such she is a good listener; in addition she is a well balanced individual with an equable temperament.

In conclusion, therefore, I can state with confidence that Charlotte will do well in whatever field of employment she puts her mind to.

Mr Brown

B20.60 Example Reference 2

25/08/2015

To whom it may concern,

I have known Charlotte Smith for the past five years and in my capacity as her teacher, I have seldom encountered such an outstanding young person. Charlotte has always shown an incredible will to learn.

I have been privileged to take Charlotte for A Level English. During this two year period she has flourished in her ability to articulate her ideas and she possesses a very high register of the language. Her perceptive qualities when analysing texts are second to none and she embodies all that is required to excel as a student in any subject. Charlotte is diligent as an independent learner and has always met any deadline set within the department.

Finally, Charlotte is one of the most polite students I have had the privilege to teach and I recommend her to any educational institution or workplace.

Regards,
Mrs Green,

Head of English, Smith College

B20.70 Project on CV's
Even if you are not currently looking for a job make sure that you have an up-to-date CV and see how you might wish to adapt this for different jobs which are advertised.

In many cases organisations also ask for a covering letter.

Think out clearly how you might relate this to your CV and keep this on your computer files if you have one.

B20.80 Project on higher education
If you're thinking of going to university it would be advisable to do this project.

Make a list of the deadlines for when you have to fill in application forms.

Example table

Name of Institution	Deadline	Comments	Grades Required
Smith University	15th September	*Great student life, but expensive accommodation.*	*A,B,C*

Name of Institution	Deadline	Comments	Grades Required
Brown University	16th September	*Keen on sport, so stress our interest in this especially Arsenal Development Centre.*	*A,B,B*
Green University	17th September	*Has writer in residence so stress interest in writing and theatre.*	*A,B,B*
Wright University	18th September	*They stress interactive tutorials so mention debating society at school.*	*A,C,C*
Jones University	19th September	*They have a very strong musical element so stress involvement in school productions as pianist.*	*A,B,B*
Carter University	22nd September	*Has a very good reputation for research so stress interest in this.*	*A,A,B*

Make a list of open days for the universities which are your ideal choices.

When thinking about universities bear in mind the type of town that you might wish to live in for three or four years. If you are not currently at school or college, it may be worthwhile purchasing a guide such as 'The Virgin Guide to British Universities'.

Make sure you have a fall-back position if you do not get to a university which is your first choice. You should be able to check fairly easily what grades the University requires for your particular course.

You might be asked for an interview and therefore it is very worthwhile thinking about what questions they might reasonably ask you. This would include why you want a particular course and why the particular university. They might also ask you about your future career hopes. You need to be fairly specific on this. There is not much point for example in saying that you want to be an economist if you have no idea what an economist does.

B20.90 Project on Interview techniques for education
Preferably in a group try working out what questions people might ask you and also what your responses are.

They could ask why you are interested in taking the particular course, and how it relates to your chosen career.

Discuss this with your colleagues.

You could use a computer to record this or you can use your own phone. Then play back your responses and see how it could be improved.

B20.100 Obtaining work at the present time
It is difficult to find part-time work on a regular basis although sometimes small cafés or larger food shops might require people. Apart from the wages they sometimes offer discounts which can be helpful as well as bonuses, for example, a share of the tips which are offered by customers.

If you have already had work experience with an organisation before you start your college course then it may be worthwhile trying to contact them to see if they are willing to employ you in the summer months or other holidays. Some may be willing to do this since it would provide relief for holidays.

Willingness to work unsocial hours may also be an advantage and some organisations require carers. Whilst it is an unglamorous occupation caring is one of the few jobs which are widely available at the present time.

Quite often CRB checks are required which means that any offences have to be declared. This would not normally include parking offences but would include any others however long ago it happened.

This is important since many people being cared for, whether the old or young, are clearly very vulnerable. In some cases caring jobs might involve looking after people in terms of personal hygiene as well as listening to people since this is an important part of caring.

In some cases local newspapers also have a website where you can register your CV for nothing and clearly this would seem to be worthwhile since there is nothing to be lost.

B20.110 Project on local jobs
Look at the local newspaper and see what jobs are advertised. What qualifications do you need?

What are the salaries or wages offered?

Are there any perks offered e.g. staff discounts, cheap meals etc? Do they require you to have a car?

Are there any other requirements for example CRB checks?

What hours of work do they require of you and does it involve unsocial hours?

Name of job	Salary or wage offered	Cost/Time taken to get to the job	Other comments
Carer	£7.00 an hour	20 minutes by bus, £15 per week	Might require unsocial hours which might mean having to get a taxi.
Waitress	£7.50 an hour	15 minutes by bus, £15 per week or £4.00 a day	Work is seasonal. You are on call so no guaranteed wage.
Swimming bath attendant	£8.00 an hour	25 minutes walk	No public transport from my house.
Shop assistant	Minimum wage	30 minutes by train	10% staff discount on all purchases
Security guard	£9.00 an hour	20 minutes walk	Unsocial hours and slight risks involved. Also some people are wary of people in uniform.

B20.120 Suggested letter to accompany CV to prospective employer

My address line 1
My address line 2
My address line 3
My telephone no.

Prospective employers address line 1
Line 2
Line 3
Postcode   Date

For the attention of (name or department)

Dear Mr/Mrs/Ms (if you have a name – Dear Sir/Madam if not)

Re. (Job description or Vacancy with a reference if known)

Further to your recent advertisement in (insert name of newspaper, agency etc) I am pleased to enclose my CV.

If you have any queries please telephone (insert telephone number including STD code) or email me at (insert email address). Otherwise I look forward to hearing from you with a suitable date for interview.

Yours sincerely (Yours faithfully if addressed to Dear Sir/Madam)

Suggested letter to accompany CV to prospective employer

My address line 1
My address line 2
My address line 3
My telephone no.

Prospective employers address line 1
Line 2
Line 3
Postcode   Date

For the attention of (name or department)

Dear Mr/Mrs/Ms (if you have a name – Dear Sir/Madam if not)

Re. (Job description or Vacancy with a reference if known)

Further to your recent advertisement in (insert name of newspaper, agency etc) I am pleased to enclose my CV.

If you have any queries please telephone (insert telephone number including STD code) or email me at (insert email address). Otherwise I look forward to hearing from you with a suitable date for interview.

Yours sincerely (Yours faithfully if addressed to Dear Sir/Madam)

Full Christian and Surname

Module B21 Specimen
Interview with Miss Smith

B21.10 Your Business Studies course
C1 Can you tell me about how your course is organised?

C2 Why did you choose a business admin course?

C3 Can you please explain about the ways in which it is assessed?

You and the job

B21.20 Your background
Y1 Which period of history did you study and did it relate at all to the sociology course?

Y2 You mention that you have been involved in drama productions, can you tell me in what way you were involved?

Y3 You also mention about art groups, can you tell me in what way you are involved?

Y4 Can you also tell me a little about the preparation for working life course?

Explanation for this question

The employer is currently writing a course on employability for the International Association of Bookkeepers (IAB) and they have asked him to provide a course which involves helping people mainly at the post- GCSE stage (NEET's, not in education, employment or training). The IAB has suggested that it would involve not just finding jobs but also to help people to adjust to life away from the family home.

Y5 What have you been doing since you left school which might help you in any way in the future?

B21.30 Word-processing and IT skills
W1 What skills have you learnt that we can use for producing material e.g. clip art, computer graphics, Excel?

W2 Have you ever used Skype and did you find it helpful?

Explanation for this question

The employer produces training packages and wishes to expand into the international market using the books and other materials which have already been published. Using Skype, having sent the materials would be a cost effective method of getting into this market.

W3 How good are you at word processing?

Explanation for this question

The employer assumes that it is helpful for an apprentice to have more paper qualifications and that a certificate which can verify that the apprentice has good ICT skills will help them to gain self-esteem.

W4 Are you willing to use and help me to use voice input more effectively?

Explanation for this question

Voice input has the advantage that even if the apprentice had injured their hand, or was otherwise incapacitated that they can still use the computer.

W5 Do you understand about computer filing systems? Do you understand about cross-referencing on a computer?

W6 Do you understand why it is important to keep a list of contacts and why we might want to file this on a geographical basis and also by names of the individuals and the organisations they represent?

W7 Do you understand about paper filing systems and how they can be used?

B21.40 Your role and the future
F1 Would you be interested in producing a book which would help your CV by having your name on it as the editor?

F2 Would it be sensible to think about approaching your old school if we have the IAB International Association of Bookkeepers material ready?

Explanation for this question

Many schools have the problem that whilst they can provide a suitable education not everyone gets jobs after school and also in some cases the schools do not have people with enough expertise to put on new courses

F3 Would they be interested in any of the packages which we could produce e.g. for A level Economics or A level Business studies? Would they be interested in purchasing our textbooks?

F4 Would they be interested in purchasing a complete package from us which would reduce the preparation time for teachers and administrative staff?

F5 As you have artistic skills would you be able to design a poster or leaflet so that we could attract more students?

F6 Do you have any ideas how we could attract publicity from the local media when we set up our new office?

F7 Would you be interested in learning the keyboard through having piano lessons from our organisation?

F8 Do you have any suggestions for business cards perhaps using your design skills?

B21.50 Minor conditions
M1 Do you have a bank account?

Explanation for this question

It is helpful to us if we can pay your wages and any incidental expenses directly into your bank account using BACS.

Introduction to the World of Work Synopsis

We have subdivided the modules into personal and business since this seems a logical approach. Educationalists suggest an inductive approach to education is the best one where we go from the experience of the students to the underlying principles and therefore we have put in the personal modules first.

The objective of all the modules is both to help people within schools or colleges to be faced with realistic choices which can be answered if necessary in the classroom but also to provide material which can be used by young people working on their own. Young people need to have transferable skills and some of these can be obtained by looking at the ways in which businesses approach them. It is therefore worthwhile trying to build up a portfolio of ways in which businesses have these approaches and to see which ones are effective and why, also which ones are totally misplaced.

Personal Modules Synopsis

For many people leaving home either to obtain a job or to go to college or university can be both exciting and bewildering.

Personal modules introduction	More on this in Module...
If you are not used to handling money shopping for one can be complicated. Getting value for money is not always easy.	P1 Shopping
Making sure that you eat properly is obviously sensible but is frequently not done and as the food chain scandal in 2013 has shown labelling of food has not been taken seriously by the supermarkets.	P2 Healthy Eating
There are many different financial institutions but not all of them are helpful. There have been complaints about overdraft charges being imposed which are not clear cut. There are also many ways in which fraudsters can try to obtain information and not all of these are obvious.	P3 Budgeting
Travelling can be expensive or inconvenient and it is not always obvious what the best ways of getting to or from work/college/leisure activities are.	P4 Travel

Fuel bills are increasing and are likely to increase further and a wide range of prices from the big 6 companies has made price comparisons difficult. There are alternatives to these.	P5 Fuel Bills
We can look at the ways in which people typically spend money and compare it with our own.	P6 Patterns of expenditure
Finding suitable accommodation is not always easy and often people have to compromise between travel costs and accommodation costs.	P7 Accommodation
Allowing sufficient time for different activities including exercise, shopping and work. Getting the balance right is not necessarily easy.	P8 Allocation of time
Getting into debt is a major concern for many young people.	P9 Personal finance
Many people find that the sheer size of educational institutions makes them impersonal and loneliness is a common problem. Self development is important and having a reasonable amount of self-esteem will help to overcome many problems.	P10 Self development
Often going away from home creates both opportunities to develop relationships but can also make existing relationships difficult.	P11 Relationships
Presentation skills are important in many courses and also for interviews. There is no easy way of acquiring these but there are techniques which can help.	P12 Presentation skills
Apprenticeships are an alternative to conventional career routes and have become increasingly popular.	P13 Career including apprenticeships
For many people, self-employment may offer a route to success although it is easy to underestimate the problems. Even within an organisation, understanding the risks which the organisation faces is helpful.	P14 Enterprise and risks
Currently we are facing many changes, for example, with shopping patterns as well as global warming and problems with future fuel supply. To ignore these is simply to bury one's head in the sand.	P15 Planning in an age of change

Business Modules Synopsis

Young people often have a vicious cycle to overcome. Organisations want people to know about different functions of business but how can young people acquire them unless they can obtain work in the first place?

Business modules introduction	More on this in Module...
Whilst some people wish to work full time on office work, other people will find that they need to carry out office work even if their main activity is something totally different. For example, in a GP's practice a great deal of office work is involved. Building contractors will in many cases need to understand the office work involved.	B1 Office work in different sectors of a business
How an office is laid out can contribute to the efficiency or inefficiency of the organisation.	B2 Office Planning
The first impressions of an organisation are often long lasting and the reception office is therefore important.	B3 Reception office
Telecommunications in most countries are now very important but many people have experienced major problems with telecommunications. It is ironic that it is impossible to leave a message with some of the largest telecommunication companies.	B4 Telecommunications
People still use mail for a variety of purposes. It is important that people know how to write letters intelligently.	B5 Mail
There are a range of private sector organisations and people looking for jobs need to understand these.	B6 Private sector organisations
Any business involves risks and it is helpful to know what the risks are and how they can be minimised.	B7 Business risks
Many organisations have grown, although there are concerns that in some cases they have become too large.	B8 Growth of organisations
There are a variety of production methods and it is helpful to understand these.	B9 Production methods
The human relations department is the one which most young people will come across and to understand what they are doing and how they try to assess people will be helpful.	B10 Human Relations Department
Accounting in some ways can be an invisible department but we soon notice if it handles matters badly. For people who wish to be self-employed a basic knowledge of accounting is extremely helpful.	B11 Accounting
Finance is extremely important. If people had really understood finance then we would not have had the credit crunch.	B 12 Finance
Purchasing of the correct goods and services in a cost effective way is extremely important. Currently in the UK, the government has so far spent several billion on a computerised system for the NHS without any obvious benefits.	B13 Purchasing
Marketing is an important part of many organisations. If it is done properly and ethically it can help society.	B 14 Marketing

The distribution of goods is rapidly changing with globalisation and also with online shopping. It therefore affects us both as consumers and also in terms of likely jobs.	B15 Distribution of goods
Organisation and methods are important to ensure that organisations act efficiently.	B16 Organisation and methods
Knowing about reliable sources of information is helpful for most jobs. Many people suggest that we are living in a 'dis-information age' i.e. that there is a lot of propaganda. Information from the media is not always accurate and we need to know how to test it.	B17 Sources of information
Business meetings occupy a large part of many organisations and if they are well thought out they can be effective, but if not they can be both a waste of money and lead to low morale of the people involved.	B18 Business meetings
Arranging visits is important for many people visiting the office.	B19 Arranging visits
Currently looking for jobs is of major importance.	B 20 Looking for jobs
Interview technique is also very helpful and many people need help with this.	B21 Specimen interview with Miss Smith